Use your research to make a c argu

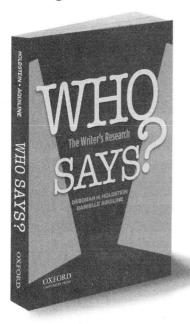

So What? The Writer's Argument shows students HOW to write compelling arguments and explains WHY the practice of argumentation is essential to their academic work.

Package and Save! Save your students 20% when you pair *Who Says?* with *So What?*. Order using package ISBN: 978-0-19-937204-1.

Who Says?

The
Writer's
Research

Deborah H. Holdstein
Columbia College Chicago

Danielle Aquiline
Oakton Community College

New York   Oxford
Oxford University Press

Oxford University Press is a department of the University of Oxford.
It furthers the University's objective of excellence in research, scholarship,
and education by publishing worldwide.

Oxford   New York
Auckland   Cape Town   Dar es Salaam   Hong Kong   Karachi
Kuala Lumpur   Madrid   Melbourne   Mexico City   Nairobi
New Delhi   Shanghai   Taipei   Toronto

With offices in
Argentina   Austria   Brazil   Chile   Czech Republic   France   Greece
Guatemala   Hungary   Italy   Japan   Poland   Portugal   Singapore
South Korea   Switzerland   Thailand   Turkey   Ukraine   Vietnam

For titles covered by Section 112 of the US Higher Education
Opportunity Act, please visit www.oup.com/us/he for the
latest information about pricing and alternate formats.

Published in the United States of America by
Oxford University Press
198 Madison Avenue, New York, NY 10016
http://www.oup.com

Oxford is a registered trade mark of Oxford University Press.

Library of Congress Cataloging-in-Publication Data

Holdstein, Deborah H., 1952-
  Who says? : the Writer's research / Deborah Holdstein, Columbia College Chicago ;
Danielle Aquiline, Oakton Community College.
     pages cm
  Includes bibliographical references and index.
  ISBN 978-0-19-994735-5
 1. Research—Methodology—Study and teaching (Higher)—Handbooks, manuals, etc.
 2. Report writing—Study and teaching (Higher)—Handbooks, manuals, etc.
 3. Academic writing—Handbooks, manuals, etc. I. Aquiline, Danielle. II. Title.
  LB2369.H64   2013
  378.007—dc23

                                                            2013030026

ISBN 978-0-19-994735-5

Printing number: 9 8 7 6 5 4 3 2 1

Printed in the United States of America
on acid-free paper

contents

Contents

Contents

preface

IN 2008, *THE ATLANTIC* published Nicholas Carr's "Is Google Making Us Stupid?," in which the author argues that our frequent use of the Internet is causing physiological changes to our brains, with great impact on the way we read and engage with texts. The piece seemed to strike a chord, quickly becoming popular; the piece was later anthologized in *The Best American Science Writing*. In explaining how his own reading habits and abilities have noticeably changed, Carr notes, "Once I was a scuba diver in the sea of words. Now I zip along the surface like a guy on a jet ski."

We have been using this metaphor as a touchstone to address the ways in which *Who Says? The Writer's Research* will engage in the kinds of conversations necessary for contemporary first-year writing classrooms and beyond—conversations missing from current research textbooks. Carr's metaphor has helped us shape our book, and it speaks, we think, to the varying challenges faced by current writing students (and, in turn, writing teachers). Namely, how does accountable, rich, and scholarly research exist alongside technologies like Google and Wikipedia that often oversimplify information? And, further, how can we push our students to engage deeply with scholarly resources when they are becoming increasingly involved—or, debilitated, as Carr seems to argue—by their own engagement with new media?

As the title *Who Says?* indicates, we are interested in helping students grapple with how and when they rely on source material to synthesize their own ideas. *Who Says?* intends to get students thinking about questions of authority and ownership and about what it means to do research writing in an age when we are all bombarded by collaborative information via databases such as Wikipedia. We want our students to not only be smart in the ways in which they approach writing but also in the ways in which they approach reading and sourcing information.

Through our own experiences as instructors, we note that many students still seem to leave our first-year writing classes with little if any notion of why we conduct or write about research to begin with. Unlike many of the books we have used and read, *Who Says?* synthesizes the strengths of each of these books—and foster students' synthesis of ideas—rather than offer the kind of "cut and paste" strategy so often present in many research textbooks. The first several chapters of *Who Says?* also engages in global conversations about the nature of research writing, addressing as well the writer's important role in academic conversations. In addition, each chapter in the book is punctuated by a section entitled "Ideas into Practice."

Who Says? is primarily intended for use in first-year writing courses, but we see its relevance to writing-intensive and writing-in-the-disciplines courses as well. It's important to note, however, what we cannot accomplish in a volume intended to be brief and readily accessible: detailed information about incorporating multimedia resources into research projects (particularly since such information becomes dated so quickly); information about specific research methodologies or discipline-specific techniques that are more appropriately conveyed by the course instructor; the many complex nuances of Internet searches, as it would be impossible to address every database and every search engine (especially as they are sometimes ephemeral); and the entire range of bibliographical citation formats, although we do delineate the major formats and point writers toward currently reliable online sources. And while we spend a good deal of time emphasizing the formulation of a strong argument and thesis and the accountability with which they are defended, this is not an argument book per se, as this is well beyond the purview of this volume.

Instead, *Who Says?* offers student writers a companion to in-class and instructor-assigned work toward the preparation of a successful and accountable research paper. It's concise, with checklists and bullet points—along with careful explanation, where appropriate—and aims to accompany other texts and valuable work in a given course and afterward.

acknowledgments

WE APPRECIATE OUR COLLEAGUES AT Oxford University Press, USA, notably Frederick Speers, whose enthusiasm for this project and for our authorship deserves (and receives) our gratitude. We also thank Carrie Brandon for her support, along with Talia Benamy, Frederick Speers' assistant. It is a privilege to work with OUP.

Columbia College Chicago and Oakton Community College also loom large in their support for this book, and we thank the numerous colleagues who directly or indirectly offered access to photocopiers, scanners, and the like.

Our personal thank-yous are profound and simple: Deborah and Danielle thank Jay Boersma and Sona Patel, respectively, for deep and unyielding support for any and all projects and ventures.

We also wish to acknowledge Craighton Berman for his inspired Sketchnote illustrations found throughout the book. We also thank David Gilman for his help with the index.

As is the custom of a credible publisher, OUP consulted with colleagues at diverse institutions across the United States for their feedback on this project. We, too, would also like to thank the following reviewers whose insights helped guide us through the revision process: Kathryn T. Adams, Allan Hancock College; Lynn Alexander, University of Tennessee-Martin; Deborah Coxwell Teague, Florida State University; Jeanne Daningburg, Roberts Wesleyan College; Jason DePolo, North Carolina A&T State University; Emily Dial-Driver, Rogers State University; Anthony Edgington, University of Toledo; Kim Gainer, Radford University; Blake Hobby, University of North Carolina-Asheville; Kathleen Mollick, Tarleton State University; Robin Lee Mozer, University of Louisville; Van Piercy, Lone Star

College-Tomball; Alison Reynolds, University of Florida; Cary D. Ser, Miami Dade College-Kendall; Keith Sisson, University of Memphis; Marilyn Stachenfeld, Saddleback College; Colette Tennant, Corban University; and Matthew Wilsey-Cleveland, University of Colorado, Boulder.

CHAPTER one

What Is Information

> The Internet is the world's largest library. It's just that all the
> books are on the floor.
> —*John Allen Paulos*

If you peruse a variety of websites, including that of the University of Rhode Island Library (http://www.uri.edu/library/staff_pages/kinnie/lib120/info.html), you will see how difficult it is to find agreement on the definition of *information*, as the following three quotes from that site indicate:

> All ideas, facts and imaginative works of the mind which have been communicated, recorded, published and/or distributed formally or informally in any format.
> —*American Library Association*

> In the beginning there was information. The word came later. The transition was achieved by the development of organisms with the capacity for selectively exploiting this information in order to survive and perpetuate their kind.
> —*Fred Dreske, Knowledge and the Flow*
> *of Information (Bedford Books, 1981)*

> Data becomes information only when it's put into a context.
> —*John McChesney, National Public Radio reporter*

Information and Being Literate about Information

As citizens and as consumers, it is essential that we become articulate investigators (some might say "critical thinkers") of that which is represented as information, especially allegedly accurate, authoritative information. This is what the term "information literacy" is about. For instance, if, indeed, the poet Gertrude Stein was correct in saying, "Everybody gets so much information all day long that they lose their common sense," it is even more striking that this statement was attributed to Stein (according to a website that we shall not mention) as having been said in 1959.

This is interesting for a couple of reasons, and it illustrates the importance of being literate about information. First, as you can imagine, the "information overload," as it is commonly called, has only increased exponentially since 1959, and even more so since the advent of the Internet, so Stein's words (if, indeed, they are) ring especially true today. The second reason: Stein died in 1946, making it impossible for her to have pronounced much of anything in 1959.

This tells us two significant things about information and the importance of being literate when confronted with various types of information, and about this information in particular. First, there is difference among information, accurate information, and real knowledge. And, second, there is always a need to attribute and cite information accurately and carefully.

The United States National Forum on Information Literacy defines "information literacy" as "the ability to know when there is a need for information, to be able to identify, locate, evaluate, and effectively use that information for the issue or problem at hand" (infolit.org, United States Government). This is in great measure what *Who Says?* is about.

While the philosophical distinctions among information literacy, information, and knowledge are perhaps beyond our purpose here, we have written *Who Says? A Writer's Research* to help you begin the important process of writing about topics that require research. This book will accompany the wisdom of your instructor and other documents or texts she or he might choose for your course and assignment, and it is not meant to be a comprehensive, highly detailed manifesto on any and all forms of research writing. (Indeed, you will note that we often use the words "research essay" and "research paper" interchangeably, even though the former represents a more personal type of research project and the latter represents a more academic research venture. We want to be inclusive of the varieties of assignments you might encounter.)

Being Overwhelmed—This Is a Process?

All types of research—whether a major, federally funded project or a term paper assignment—are characterized by a process, that is, a set of procedures or methods by which the research assignment, in this case, is carried out.

For instance, you've likely heard about the process for scientific research, by which scientists establish a problem, examine aspects of the problem using prior information, create a hypothesis, compose a research methodology, and then set about proving (and sometimes disproving) the hypothesis. Your task, while not necessarily scientific, is similar: As you will see as you go through these chapters and use the guidance of your instructor, you will examine what interests you; ways to center and focus what interests you; see what information has been established by others who are interested in the topic; perhaps create your own, relevant research materials (such as interviews, if appropriate for your investigation); craft an argument; and prove that argument in writing.

This is to say that while you might be feeling overwhelmed by the laundry list of tasks that lay ahead, the good news is that there is, in fact, a process—a series of tried and true steps that, no matter how recursive or repetitive they may seem, are steps that you eventually will incorporate into the idiosyncrasies and complexities of your own research project. In learning any new process, you might find these steps cumbersome; however, we find that they become second nature after a while, and you will find your comfort level increase as you become more intellectually secure with and accountable for the complexities of your project.

This book is therefore intended as a supportive guide, one to accompany you as you begin to think about and to formulate a topic, generate resources, craft a thesis/statement of purpose, and fulfill the other obligations of an appropriately documented, well-crafted written research project. We hope that you will use the *information* you gather on your particular topic to generate *knowledge*, as you discern between that which is useful, credible, and appropriate for your audience and for the work that you intend to do.

Ideas Into Practice

This is one of many ways to develop a game plan and time line for your research and writing. After all, it's always good to have a game plan, and the research process is no different.

With the help of the deadlines and other requirements set by your instructor, create a time line for your work, whether it's on hard copy in a notebook or on your smartphone or laptop calendar. First, create a list of milestones; this might include "determine topic," "vet sources," "craft thesis," "create annotated bibliography," "annotated bibliography due for class discussion," and so forth. If one of your entries is "find topic by September 30," you'll likely want to insert into your calendar (print or otherwise) a reminder two weeks before that deadline.

Work with your fellow classmates and your instructor to determine and record milestones that will be common to everyone, adapting them and your own work habits to ensure that your work is completed well and on time.

CHAPTER two

Says Who? The Writer's Authority, the Writer's Voice

talking points

- How does the rhetorical situation affect the way I approach my work?
- What is *ethos*?
- Why is my ethos as a researcher important?
- What helps me to establish my ethos? How can my ethos be damaged?
- What is voice?
- Where does my voice as a writer come in?
- Does my diction matter?

We would like you to think about the various situations in which you might be asked to produce written text, situations that will almost certainly extend beyond the classroom. Clearly, these points are likely useful to you for your research writing in addition to other occasions for writing. Because you will likely be asked to do many types of writing for many different audiences throughout both your educational and professional careers, it is important that you always consider *the rhetorical situation* for which you are writing.

The Rhetorical Situation

The rhetorical situation—a concept attributed to Aristotle—asks us to consider the following when composing a written text: the writer, the audience, the purpose, the topic, and the occasion. Let's break this down even further and take a look at the kinds of questions that will help you address each of those elements.

Considering the Writer—Or, as Aristotle Put It, the Speaker

Who is the speaker? How does she or he convey authority? Does the speaker work to develop ethos? What is the experience of the speaker and how does that experience award the speaker credibility?

Considering the Audience—Your Readers

Who is the target audience for your argument? What does the audience expect? Does the audience consist of experts in the field of study? Will the audience be evaluating the written text in any way? What is the audience's relationship to the writer?

Considering the Purpose—In Addition to Fulfilling the Assignment

Is the piece of writing meant to convey a message? Make a point? Entertain? Delight? Praise? Criticize? Analyze? Is the writing trying to persuade us of something? What is the goal?

Considering the Topic—Larger Issues

Is the tone of the writing appropriate for this topic? What are the specific conventions for the particular discipline in which you are writing? Does the writing provide the necessary context for the argument being made?

Considering the Occasion

Why is this piece of writing being composed? In what context will this writing be presented? What are the expectations and standard conventions of that particular context? What is the setting for this writing (time, place, etc.)?

These considerations lead to our discussion of *ethos*.

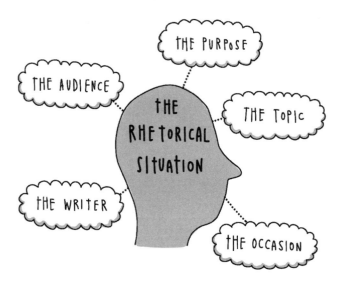

Establishing Ethos

In addition to the rhetorical situation, we think it's important to remember that research writing is an intellectual activity. What we're thinking about won't necessarily transmit a specific set of skills, but we hope to make you aware of the larger contexts for writing and for writing the results of your research.

To further contextualize this conversation, we need to talk a bit more about *rhetoric*. So let's do it this way:

> *Quick Fact*
> Aristotle defined rhetoric as the "art of persuasion" and identified three primary rhetorical modes: pathos, logos, and ethos.

For the purpose of this discussion, we'll have to be satisfied with rather quick definitions. Although we'll talk primarily about ethos, let us introduce you to these basic concepts (see Table 2.1).

Table 2.1   THE THREE MAIN FORMS OF RHETORIC

Pathos—Appealing to the audience on the basis of emotion.	**Logos**—Appealing to the audience on the basis of logic.	**Ethos**—Appealing to the audience on the basis of one's character and implied, guiding beliefs.
Beliefs Feelings Emotion Subjectivity	Logic Reason Fact Objectivity	Reputation Trustworthiness Authority Credibility

Let's put some of this into action. Let's say that you want to persuade your family that you should be given an all-expense-paid trip to Europe next summer. (We know. This is just an exercise, remember?)

Now, make an appeal to your parents, using each of the three forms of rhetoric: pathos, logos, and ethos.

Using Pathos

"But all my friends are going, and don't you want me to have important life experiences?" or "Do you want me to be the only one of my friends who doesn't get to go on this trip?"

Using Logos

"Sixty percent of students who travel abroad are more readily accepted into professional and graduate schools. I have documented evidence that an overseas experience will not only increase the depth and breadth of my knowledge, but also that it will provide the kind of cross-cultural benefits that employers look for these days."

Demonstrating Ethos

"I've received good grades all of last year, and I'm on the Honor Roll. I've proven myself to be personally responsible, as my exemplary behavior during spring break last year amply illustrates. I'm responsible, I can multitask and experience the world while getting my work done, and I'm dedicated to making you and our family proud."

Let us emphasize that your real-life situations will, of course, be far more nuanced and not nearly this simple. You'll likely be relying on a combination of these forms for your arguments, whether for your parents or for your writing.

However, we want you to be most mindful of your ethos, because both pathos and logos, depending on how these are demonstrated, both affect your ethos—that is, the good character you project as a credible speaker or writer. To put it even more simply, does your targeted audience have good reason to believe or want to follow the argument you are making?

Ways to Damage Your Ethos

Sometimes the little things—or, rather, things that seem little to you—can have a tremendous impact on your ability to impress or persuade your reader and could potentially undermine your *ethos*.

Let's say you're watching a press conference featuring a prominent politician. He or she is less than prepared and seems evasive when asked questions that would have seemed to be central to the reason for the conference in the first place. This might indicate to you that either the politician is refusing to answer honestly—or that the politician just doesn't know the answer. What would be your reaction? Such stances clearly damage the ethos of the speaker. Would it help your perception of the politician for him or her to have simply said, "I cannot answer this question because I do not yet know the answer," rather than trying to be evasive? For most of us, yes.

The point here is that even if you previously haven't heard of the word *ethos*, you might have called into question the credibility of the politician. You are aware of speakers' trustworthiness and your perception of that trustworthiness even if you haven't been aware of the Greek term for "character."

Let's think about how this figures into your ethos as a writer.

For instance, if you rely too heavily on source materials (the kind of "patchwriting" we'll discuss later on in these pages), you may communicate that you as a research writer don't fully understand and can't support your own argument without back-to-back quoting of others. On the other hand, if you present information that isn't cited carefully—and that isn't common knowledge—your audience will question how you know this information and will begin to suspect that you might be plagiarizing or, at the very least, that you do not know how to document appropriately and properly.

If your article isn't formatted appropriately, if it doesn't follow the format or the appropriate conventions of the discipline in which you're writing, these issues also complicate and undermine your credibility as a writer and thinker.

In the end, think also about the signs and signals that mark a credible source as you conduct research and the things you see that might discredit a particular source, thus damaging your own credibility. For example, consider a Web page that is completely user-made without documented, research-worthy materials. Using this as an authoritative source potentially makes you less than authoritative, unless, of course, your topic is "wonky websites."

Again, although you may not be familiar with the term *ethos*, you likely are well able to identify or discern a credible website in the first five to ten seconds of the site's loading on your screen, further indicating that there is a variety of nuanced signals that audiences note and use to conclude whether a website, politician, or research paper is credible and authoritative. It's your voice that comes through that research paper—and it's your ethos that is conveyed through your voice and choice of diction.

Voice and Writing

When we speak of "voice," we don't mean the way you sound when you speak. Instead, we're talking about the unique way that you convey your individual style as a writer. Many factors come into the reader's sense of your voice: your word choice (diction), your turn of phrase (your syntax), or the sophistication of your vocabulary (and knowing when not to sound overinflated or deliberately obscuring).

Think of the blogs you read regularly, for example. In an era of online text, bloggers must work especially hard to hone their individual voices; they must write in a way that both effectively communicates their personalities and sets them apart from the sea of other bloggers with whom they are competing for your readership.

We are both avid readers of food blogs and can readily identify our favorite bloggers by their written voices. In fact, it is often the voice—the choices these writers have made in the way they write—that attract us to their blogs in the first place, and it's the voice that keeps us coming back time and time again. Their voices are distinctively *theirs*. That is, they are easily identifiable and help us, the readers, better understand who each person is as a writer (or food blogger) and what she or he wants us to understand as readers (or foodie fans).

Consider this example from the popular blog, *Smitten Kitchen* (www.smittenkitchen.com):

> *It's the first week of January, so I am going to go out on a limb and guess that no fewer than 52 percent of you are gnawing on a carrot stick right now. If you're not gnawing on a carrot stick right now, you probably have some within reach of you. If they're not within reach of you, they're in your fridge, because you, like most of us, are more ambitious when it comes to grocery lists than you might be when it's time to consume said groceries. And if they're not in your fridge, you might have them on your mind, nagging at you. Early January is like that. (Late January is all about rich comfort foods. Trust me.)*
> *(January, 2013)*

In this excerpt from this very successful blog, writer Deb Perelman demonstrates a certain "I know you, you trust me, and I'm your best buddy" voice that has—in addition to outstanding recipes and a compelling "backstory" ("Regular Woman Works Miracles in Tiny Manhattan Kitchen," the headline might read)—contributed to her success. Perelman knows that even if you do not find yourself "gnawing on a carrot stick," even if you don't have any in your refrigerator, as she seems to assume, you will intuitively understand what it means for her to begin this part of her blog by stating, "It's the first week in January." What does that mean to most readers? Probably the post-holiday slump of back to work in (often) terrible weather, (for many) cold temperatures, and a desire to hibernate until spring. Perlman doesn't need to say all this, of course: she assumes you, the reader, get it, even if her assumptions about you are incorrect. And because her voice is so familiar, when the excerpt ends with a request that you trust her, it's likely that you will; and even if you're not sure, you'll likely give the recipe a try (and *then* you'll trust her). Perelman's voice reveals warmth, closeness, and an intelligent, welcoming friendship—an intimate acquaintance who's talking with you across the kitchen table.

Of course, it's unlikely that you will be writing for an audience of foodies who you'll be able to assume are your best friends—ever. Nonetheless, it is still important that, when conceiving your writing and your paper, that you be mindful of your audience and your purpose so that your voice is appropriate for your particular rhetorical situation. Depending on the subject and writer, another blog, of course, will have a completely different tone and effect on the reader. In research writing, and again, depending on the discipline or genre in which you're writing, your voice may come across as personal or too personal; stiff or not stiff enough; scholarly or too informal. You get the picture.

Let's say that you want to communicate to several people the fact that you're under the weather and will have to miss class. The way in which you communicate this will depend not only on the medium and genre of your communication but also on your targeted audience:

For the instructor, via e-mail:

> *Dear Professor Hogwash: I'm really sorry, but I'm running a fever, and I won't be able to be in class today. I will follow the syllabus, and I will be sure to prepare this assignment for our next class, and if it is acceptable to you, I will also turn in the work that we were to have done in class today. As we are advised on the syllabus, I will also contact a classmate to see if there is anything new that comes in class today. Sincerely, Smart Student*

For a classmate/friend, via text message:

> *Hey. Dipping stats today. Txt me aftr Hog's class with info and hw.   Ttyl.*

Clearly, you would not, we trust, use text-messaging-appropriate or informal language when communicating with your instructor.

Now, these are extreme examples, but as with the exercise regarding the different forms of rhetoric, your voice depends on your targeted audience and the medium and level of diction (word choice) you invoke. These are decisions that you make on a daily basis, but we'd like you to be mindful of these choices, especially as they have an impact on your research and your writing. Part of your job as a writer—and part of your responsibility in making your essay readable, persuasive, and cohesive—is to find the proper voice with which you will write. Doing so is often a balance, not between the extremes we illustrated earlier, but rather in knowing how to use appropriate word choice and the style that's expected in the genre and discipline in which you are writing, balancing citation with your own use of language. Keep in mind, of course, that each of your sources will have the author's own distinct voice, so your primary struggle will be to ensure that your voice as a research writer sets an appropriate tone for your paper.

Owning Your Voice

In the process of integrating their source materials, some students lose sight of their own distinct voices and their own arguments. The important point is this: although you are looking to researchers and scholars to help you construct your argument, this is ultimately your work and your research writing should represent who you are both as an academic and as a writer. We treat this topic further elsewhere in this book.

Ideas Into Practice

Think of the example we gave you about your request to spend the summer in Europe. In that example, we asked you to use each of the three rhetorical forms in an attempt to persuade. Now, choose one of the research topics from the following list and enact a similar exercise in which you try to persuade your audience using these three forms. Therefore, in this activity, proceed as follows:

> After choosing the topic, take a stand on that topic. Remember that your stand must be something that can be argued—it cannot suggest a "yes" or "no" response. Consider your audience. What do you need to do to appeal to that particular audience or set of audiences?

> As an intellectual exercise, make an appeal using each of the three rhetorical forms—*ethos, logos, pathos*—as discussed in this chapter.

This is an opportunity to try out your research skills, which we will discuss elsewhere in this book, as you find the best examples with which to argue your point of view. The topics: *These are deliberately controversial (and somewhat hackneyed, but not necessarily unimportant) topics, ones that your instructor might dissuade you from choosing for your research paper. (And we'll leave that to the instructor to explain.)*

Marijuana legalization
Abortion rights
Gun control
Euthanasia
Animal rights

CHAPTER three

But You Said This Was Collaborative: Plagiarism

talking points

- What is plagiarism?
- How do I know when I'm plagiarizing?
- I can just change the words, right?
- What are the various forms of plagiarism?
- How do I document the information if it can be considered common knowledge? Should I still account for it?
- What are some ways to avoid plagiarism?

In Chapter 2, you have read a great deal about determining who you are as a writer and how you can work to establish your *ethos*—your credibility as a researcher. It is important that you realize that your ethos is dependent not only on what ideas you contribute to academic conversations but also on how indebted and accountable you are to the ideas that came before you. In many ways, this is the dance that all researchers must do: balancing the work they are doing with the work that others—often many others—have already done.

17

Understanding Plagiarism

It is amidst this choreography that students often get caught in the trap of plagiarism. Intentionally or unintentionally, students will lose sight of their own voices and ideas and will, instead, misappropriate the words and language of their resources, that is, the words written and published by others.

Plagiarism occurs when you use words or ideas that are not your own and you do not cite them. In other words, you plagiarize when you do not acknowledge in appropriate ways that someone else has written words or has published ideas that you claim are yours. You plagiarize by doing the following:

- Stealing another's ideas or words and passing them off as your own
- Using resources without giving credit
- Forgetting to put quotation marks around a direct quote
- Buying an essay and turning it in as your own

Deliberate plagiarizing violates academic integrity and is nothing short of cheating. It is admitting that you—the research writer—are incapable of crafting your own essay; it is also an admission of defeat. And, in many colleges and universities, plagiarism is seen, in many ways, as a moral offense punishable by suspension or expulsion.

Regardless of whether you copy from a published or private source, a website or a magazine, an encyclopedia or an Internet forum, unless you give credit to other authors for both their ideas and their words, you have plagiarized. Be mindful, as well, of copyright laws, particularly as research projects are sometimes written as well as multimedia: graphics, photographs, music sampling, and the like are all subject to forms of copyright. You must credit all sources to avoid copyright infringement, even if you are using an image, say, only for your presentation.

Further, keep in mind that, although the Internet has certainly made it easier to find sources and essays to plagiarize, it has also made it easier for teachers to detect plagiarism. Websites such as *WriteCheck*, *TurnItIn*, and *iThenticate* have developed what some institutions and professors find to be useful tools that aid in both plagiarism detection and prevention. However, as teachers, we also recognize that students sometimes plagiarize accidentally. In most instances, the penalties—and the violation of ethics—are equally severe, even if the plagiarism is inadvertent. So, in what follows, we hope to equip you with tools that will help you to avoid the plagiarism trap.

Examples of Plagiarism

The following is an excerpt from Paul Shepard's essay, "Hunting and Human Values." We've used this passage, and the samples following, to illustrate various kinds of plagiarism. You will note, however, that in contrast to our previous advice—to put quotation marks around any borrowed passage—that a long quote such as the one we have taken from Shephard's essay is separated and indented from the rest of the text as follows, indicating that it is a quote to be attributed (not dissimilar from the kind of block quotes many citation styles require):

> *Original Text*
> Regardless of the technological advance, man remains part of a dependent upon nature. The necessity of signifying and recogniz-ing this relationship remains, though it may not seem so. The hunter is our agent of awareness. He is not only an observer but a participant and receiver. He knows that man is a member of a natural community and that the processes of nature will never become so well understood or controlled that faith will cease to be important.
>
>> *–Shepard, Paul. "Fellow Creatures."* Man in the Landscape: A Historic View of the Esthetics of Nature. *University of Georgia Press, 2002. 190–213.*
>
> *Word-for-Word Plagiarism*
> Paul Shepard suggests that the hunter is not only an observer but also a participant and receiver. The hunter knows that man is a member of a natural community and that the processes of nature will never become so well understood or controlled that faith will cease to be important.

This kind of exact copying and pasting is the most blatant form of plagiarism, even if it is unintended. Although the original author, Paul Shepard, has been acknowledged and the quote attributed to him, there has been no attempt to designate this passage as a direct quote or to document the source from which these ideas came. There should be both quotation marks around a passage of fewer than three sentences and an appropriate citation, using a recognized citation format (usually specified by your instructor).

Patchwork, or the Plagiarism Paraphrase

Man is dependent upon nature, regardless of the technological advance. Though it doesn't seem like it, the necessity of signifying and recognizing this relationship still remains. Man is not only an observer; he is also a participant and receiver (Shepard 5).

This is the kind of plagiarism to which students fall prey most often. It is important to note that, while there is a citation form (using the MLA style) here, *this passage is still plagiarized*.

Often, this sort of plagiarism is the result of inadequate paraphrasing, and that is the case here. Students may think they are translating ideas from a text into their own language, but they are really just shuffling around the text's original language. When there are three or more words linked together in the same order as the original text, such as "regardless of the technological advance" or "the necessity of signifying and recognizing the relationship still remains," the phrase should be crafted as a direct quote, with the writer surrounding the passage with quotation marks.

Idea-Based Plagiarism

The hunter is a necessity; he is our only agent of awareness. He is there to remind us that we are part of a larger natural community. No matter how technologically advanced we become, we will always be dependent on nature.

This is an example of the way particular ideas are still explicitly derived from the original text, even though the writer may have changed aspects of the language. This example also illustrates how plagiarizing extends beyond just blatant copying; idea-based plagiarism is a less explicit form of stealing, but it is unethical and irresponsible nonetheless. Therefore, just as you would with a direct quote, you must include appropriate, academic documentation that credits the author.

Avoiding Plagiarism

The first step in avoiding plagiarism involves making a commitment. Writers must commit to doing the work necessary to integrate resources properly and to use those resources to synthesize new and original ideas. Once that commitment is made, avoiding plagiarism is actually fairly simple; be a diligent note taker and a savvy editor. We can help with both of those highly nuanced tasks, and we trust that the examples from Paul Shepard's work are a start.

It's Okay to Use Resources (and It's Expected)

Using resources doesn't diminish your credibility as a writer; it actually *enhances* your credibility. *How* you use them is important.

Quite often, students fail to realize that research is a collaborative process, but it's collaborative in a variety of ways, some of which might not be anticipated. You, as the writer, are collaborating with the ideas of many others who have done similar or related work before you. And guess what? Those scholars—the very ones that *you* are citing—likely once depended on the work of others, too. This is how the conversation continues, and this is the way that academic communities operate.

When you cite resources in research writing, you demonstrate to your reader several important things:

- You have done time in the trenches. That is, you've spent hours, days, or perhaps weeks searching through online databases, thumbing through online (or, very rarely these days, hard copy) card catalogs and requesting materials, and perusing shelves or lists of books in the library. In other words, you've done your research, and appropriate documentation proves it.
- You value the academic contribution of scholars. You see worth in work done by others, and you understand that consulting the ideas of others is an integral part of formulating your own ideas.
- You are concerned about your own ethos. You want to be able to appear credible, responsible, and ethical.
- You are savvy enough to not only quote from, but to also engage with, your resources.

Therefore, don't be afraid to rely on your resources as long as you cite them properly. In subsequent chapters, we will suggest ways to make habits of good citation.

Common Knowledge

As we have written and will continue to discuss, you must cite all of the information that you find throughout the research process. This is what makes you an ethical and accountable researcher, essential qualities for building credibility with your audience.

However, what happens when, in your essay, you share information that everyone knows—facts, statistics, and stories that most people are familiar with? Should you cite those things, too? The answer can be tricky.

When you are including information in your research writing that is widely known and reported, that information could be considered *common knowledge*.

However, there are no clear boundaries or definitions for what can be considered common knowledge. And, while you wouldn't be expected to cite most of the information that qualifies as such, it is still important that you discern what is common knowledge and what is not.

You Do Not Need to Document It If. . .

- You are citing an encyclopedic piece of information that is easily verified, such as a well-known date, historical facts, birthplaces, and so on.

  Example: John F. Kennedy was assassinated on November 22, 1963.

- You are citing information that most of the general public *should* know.

  Example: There are three types of clouds: cumulus, cirrus, and stratus.

- You are citing information that has been well documented by numerous sources and that, therefore, has become general knowledge.

  Example: Michael Phelps, the Olympic swimmer, holds the record for the most Olympic gold medals.

However, if you are unsure whether an idea would be considered common knowledge, go ahead and cite the source. In the case of academic documentation, it is better to err on the side of too much rather than too little. Note cards, whether digital or hard copy, can help you keep track of these important citations.

The Art of the Note Card—Of Any Kind

Despite our general reliance on digital technologies for research, writing, record keeping, and any other host of conveniences, there are some tried-and-true methods that are delightfully low tech and might well remain so: the note card.

In fact, use of the note card can be one of a number of ways to help you avoid plagiarism.

Note cards allow you to do the following: you can summarize (rather than copy) content from your sources and accurately record in writing all aspects of the source that will readily allow you to compile your bibliography. You can create a paper note card or use the "notes" feature on your smartphone or tablet—and other, myriad possibilities. The point is to make whatever method you choose an organized one that gives you a way to record the information you need.

Therefore, while our ways of researching information have changed, our need to evaluate the suitability of a source and to document that source and cite it carefully *has not.*

Indeed, advice promulgated in 1972 by James McCrimmon in his celebrated textbook, *Writing with a Purpose* (Boston: Houghton-Mifflin, 1972), has fully transcended the test of time:

> When you begin intensive reading, you should also begin taking notes. The results of your preliminary reading may be carried in your head, but you are now beginning to collect the actual evidence from which your paper will be written, and it is important to the success of the rest of your work that both the form and the content of your notes be satisfactory. (232)

Always, and accurately, write the source on the card (or its equivalent) first; then, summarize the portion of the source that you are using, being careful to have just one such note per card or screen. If you are quoting an opinion, be sure to use quotation marks on the card, surrounding the quote, so that you remember to do the same in your paper. If you have been able to write a credible summary in your own words, you must still cite the source.

McCrimmon concisely and usefully summarizes his own recommendations regarding note taking; we therefore present them to you here, adapted with an occasional annotation in brackets to acknowledge that our ways of conducting research may have expanded and changed in recent years. The time-honored *criteria* for appropriate citation, however, have not changed, and they transcend the changes in our source materials and expanded ways of doing research. Remember, then, that we are using the word "card" expansively, denoting both its paper form and its digital equivalents:

- Put notes on cards (or individual screens, for instance, on your smartphone "notes" feature), not in notebooks [digital or paper], with one note to a card [or screen *so that you can organize and reorganize them as necessary when you craft your paper*].
- On each card identify the exact source of the note, including the page number [*if a book, or the URL or other appropriate ways to identify matter from digital sources*].
- Enclose in quotation marks the actual words of an author, whether the notes are statements of fact or of opinion.
- Summarize extensive quotations if possible, but still identify the source.
- Use direct quotation whenever the exact wording may be significant, especially if you are going to criticize a statement in the source.
- Be careful that your notes—whether direct quotations or summaries—do not distort the meaning when taken out of their original context. (McCrimmon 236)

Overall, then, keeping these points in mind, consider these tips for avoiding plagiarism:

Tips for Avoiding Plagiarism
- Have an organized system for conducting your research, including note cards, keywords, and a working bibliography.
- Use your note cards to keep track of all bibliographical information that you will later need to cite your sources.
- "Recycle" the source language twice when paraphrasing: once for your notes and then again in your essay.
- Look at your notes—not the original source—when drafting your essay.
- Check your work against the original text to be sure you haven't accidentally plagiarized.
- Make use of good citation habits, including citing your sources as you write your rough draft. Do not wait until your draft is complete or then try to work backwards, adding citations to text that is fully composed; you will make your work that much more difficult.
- When you've fallen behind on a project, don't be afraid to ask your instructor for an extension. (But be prepared for "no.")
- Read through your final draft and make sure that all necessary information is cited properly.
- Most important, give credit where credit is due!

To reiterate: using a system of note cards to track and organize your research—whether on a tablet, your smartphone, or on an index card—will make it easier for you to discern where the information came from and how you should document it appropriately in your essay. There are many note-taking applications for various electronic devices that will allow you to do what good researchers have always done: to keep thorough and thoughtful notes. We encourage you to do whatever makes you feel the most comfortable. So, if you prefer hand writing your notes, then using a traditional index card may be helpful to you (this method has, after all, worked for decades). If, however, you'd rather keep your notes on your electronic device (because, let's be honest, we all always have our smartphones or electronic tablets with us), then there are many ways for you to do that effectively.

Ideas Into Practice

As we have discussed, good note taking is the first step in avoiding plagiarism. It is also useful, front-end work, and it is a part of the research process that will help tremendously when you write your paper and create your bibliography. It is not only important that you keep track of all of your bibliographical information, but it is also essential that you keep clear and precise record of whether the information you've written is directly quoted, paraphrased, or a product of our own ideas.

Regardless of the medium you choose for your note cards, consider modeling your notes after the ones in the illustration. When note taking, be sure to include the following: title of the source; author's name; page number; the information you want to remember; and, perhaps most important, whether the information is paraphrased, summarized, or directly quoted. Remember: Although it may seem cumbersome to do all of this note taking now, it will save you a lot of work once you begin writing and as you prepare your final draft.

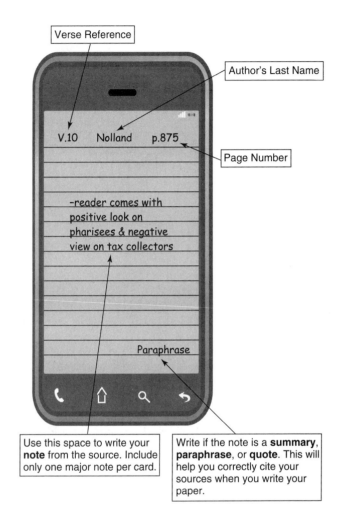

Verse Reference

Author's Last Name

V.10   Nolland   p.875

Page Number

-reader comes with positive look on pharisees & negative view on tax collectors

Paraphrase

Use this space to write your **note** from the source. Include only one major note per card.

Write if the note is a **summary**, **paraphrase**, or **quote**. This will help you correctly cite your sources when you write your paper.

CHAPTER four

Who Cares?
Identifying
the Problem

talking points

- What should I write about?

- How do I turn my big idea into a narrowed research topic?

- Why should I consider the audience when conceiving of a topic?

- Do I still need to have a thesis?

- What's the difference between a topic and an argument?

If you're reading this book, it is likely that you are in a writing class in which the instructor requires that you write a research essay. Your instructor has walked you through academic documentation, given you tours of the library and online resources, and has left you with three, perhaps terrifying, words: *choose a topic*.

Finding a Topic

Selecting a research topic is, for many students, one of the most daunting tasks in academic writing. It is also, as we tell our students, the single most important decision you'll make in the research writing process.

Not only will your decision determine whether your essay is received by an interested and invested audience, but it will also inform the scholarly work that you do for the next several weeks (and possibly for several months). You don't want to find yourself spending long nights in the library and online, researching something that doesn't interest you and that doesn't have an impact on those around you. Therefore, you need to choose your topic wisely.

If you are just starting your project, you will need to begin thinking through possible research topics that interest you.

Here are a few steps that you will consider in this chapter. We will ask that you:

First: Identify a list of subjects that interest you.
Next: Use *pre-searching* both to help you survey what resources are available to you and to help you further explore your broad interests.
Then: Focus your idea by narrowing your research subject into a workable, appropriate research topic.

Start with a Subject

It's perfectly acceptable to begin by thinking very broadly. In fact, the process of selecting a research topic can be represented visually as a funnel, such as the one you see in the illustration. You will start with a big idea and, through several processes that you'll read about in this chapter, you should be on your way to a narrowed and focused research question.

Provided that your instructor hasn't directed you to write about one topic in particular, your research subject can be inspired by a variety of factors, including both your personal interests and your favorite areas of study.

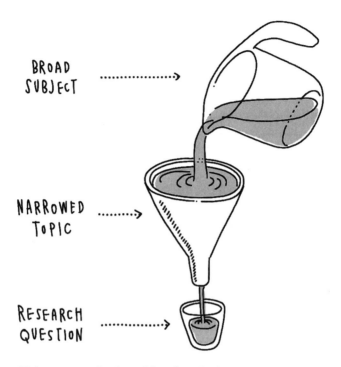

BROAD
SUBJECT   ·············>

NARROWED
TOPIC   ········>

RESEARCH
QUESTION   ·············>

To begin, compile a list of these broad subjects. Your list may look something like this:

Adoption
Rain forests
Fashion
Film
Music
Politics
Computers
Sports
World War II
Mahatma Gandhi

These subjects are not unlike topic headings that you would find in the library, and—as we've already mentioned—they can be general; don't be afraid to start big. These broad interests will serve as the umbrellas under which you will develop more narrowed topics and, eventually, a focused research question. Eventually, you will need to *argue a point of view* about your topic, one that you can prove with the resources available to you.

It is sometimes helpful to think about *conceptual* versus *practical* problems in research, as the conceptual problem, once the problem or topic is narrowed, is often more appropriate in humanities-related subjects than is the practical problem, more an appropriate scheme in scientific areas.

Practical versus Conceptual Research Problems

Here's a *practical problem*: How do we improve the quality of drinking water in developing countries?
Certain disciplines lend themselves more readily to practical problems than others. For instance, many scientific problems pose a hypothesis, for which a solution is then found. Some scientific problems also lend themselves to quantitative data and analysis.

Here's a *conceptual problem*: Why did the Democrats win the White House in 1960?
The conceptual problem doesn't have a readily tangible result; the "solution" is often disputable, and therefore an appropriate argument—citing appropriate, relevant sources—must be made.

We are looking at a problem that lends itself to more qualitative research, leading to additional questions that will form the basis for research. So, for instance, you might ask the further question, "How did the first televised Presidential debate in 1960 change the outcome of the 1960 Presidential election?"

Pre-Searching

When our students have first been assigned a research project and are beginning to think through possible topics of interest, we often encourage them to do a little digging before they finalize their research questions. This *pre-searching*, as we call it, usually involves conducting a few searches, both on the Internet and in library databases, using some of the broader subjects as keywords. These pre-searches serve two primary purposes.

First, especially when pre-searching library databases, you will be able to survey how many relevant resources—that is, resources that may be useful to you for your respective research topics—are available in your college or local library. The accessibility of applicable resources should be a factor when determining whether you have chosen the right topic. We always tell our students to set themselves up for success, and one of the ways to do this is to assure that the resources necessary for your project are readily available to you.

Consequently, you'll want to ask yourself several questions as you sift through your pre-search findings on several possible subjects:

How many books does my school library have about horror films?

Do I have access to any periodicals (journals, magazines, etc.) and other, credible online sources that may include articles about hip-hop music?

What resources are available under the subject heading "child psychology?"

Finding answers to these questions now, and identifying valuable resources before you decide on your final research question, will streamline some of the work you will encounter throughout your research process. It might also save frustration down the line if you realize that several resources that you'd expected to find might not be available to you after all.

We also encourage our students to conduct pre-searches because, in addition to helping them survey available resources, these searches also help them to recognize and identify certain specific areas of interest within their subjects—something like "things I found on my way to looking up something else."

You may, for example, know that you'd like to research American snack foods for your project. While that is a good start (and it illustrates that you are, indeed, thinking broadly to start), it is also a very large subject, and you will, ultimately, need to determine what point you will argue about snack foods. However, through some pre-searching—either by sifting through online articles or thumbing through the contents of a book—you may come to find a small facet of that subject that interests you. Perhaps you'll end up writing about how Twinkies changed in the face of World War II. Or perhaps you'll get caught up in the tale of the Wrigley chewing gum company and its influence on advertising.

Either way, the point is that pre-searching will likely lead to some information that you didn't know before or hadn't expected to find. And that information may lead you away from topics that have already been written about extensively and instead lead you toward a topic that is both new and interesting for you and your audience alike.

Moving from a Subject to a Topic

Once you have your list of subjects that interest you, it is time to begin narrowing them down to possible research topics. As we've already discussed, research subjects are usually broad and unfocused. They often take the shape of one-word terms or phrases: politics, sports, film, sports and the economy, and the like. Your topic, instead, should begin to identify what *aspect* of your subject is most interesting to you.

One of the best ways to begin this process of focusing is by listing those aspects that you find most intriguing. Go subject by subject and ask yourself, "What is it *about* politics or sports or film that I find so interesting?" This sort of brainstorming should push you beyond just identifying a general area of interest, and it should help you approach your research topic with much more specificity.

In addition, when moving from a subject of interest to a focused research topic, make use of the resources you find while pre-searching. When you begin exploring resources in the library, you will notice that the layers of depth within the library's database, in many ways, parallel the layers of depth you will be discovering throughout the process of developing a research topic. You begin with a broad subject, and these subjects are often very similar to the Library of Congress subject headings that we use to catalog texts.

For example, let's take a look at what we find in a library catalog when searching for fashion. As you can see from the screenshot, that

#	Number of Titles	Heading (Click to see titles.)	Heading Type
See Also 1	230	Fashion.	Library of Congress
2	2	Fashion.	General Heading
3	7	Fashion.	Sears list of subject headings
4	2	Fashion--20th century.	Library of Congress
5	1	Fashion--20th century--Exhibitions.	Library of Congress
6	13	Fashion 20th century History.	Library of Congress
7	4	Fashion--20th century--Pictorial works.	Library of Congress
8	1	Fashion--21st century.	Library of Congress
9	1	Fashion--21st century--Exhibitions.	Library of Congress
10	1	Fashion--21st century--Pictorial works.	Library of Congress
See Also 11	0	Fashion accessories	Library of Congress
See Also 12	0	Fashion Advertising	Library of Congress
13	3	Fashion--Africa.	Library of Congress
14	1	Fashion--Africa--20th century--Exhibitions.	Library of Congress
15	2	Fashion--Africa--Pictorial works.	Library of Congress
16	1	Fashion--Africa--Social aspects.	Library of Congress
17	1	Fashion--Africa, Sub-Saharan.	Library of Congress
18	1	Fashion and architecture.	Library of Congress
19	1	Fashion and architecture--History--21st century.	Library of Congress
20	23	Fashion and art.	Library of Congress

There are numerous Library of Congress subject headings for Fashion. Identifying the subject headings for the various subjects that interest you may help you identify a research topic.

broad subject heading—"fashion"—is widely represented; there are over 200 titles in this library that fall under this general subject.

However, you'll also see that there are several similar subject headings that may interest you, and these new subjects (Fashion—Africa, Fashion and architecture, Fashion and art) may help you define further what exactly it is you would like to research for your essay. (And, clearly, even these somewhat more defined subjects are still very broad and will require that you further specify them.)

If you click on the available titles for "fashion" and begin to survey the titles available, as we encourage you to do when you are pre-searching, you will start to see that the titles offer you keywords, topics, and ideas for your research paper.

Take a look at the screenshot, which shows some of the titles available in this particular library.

#	Subject Heading	Full Title	Date	Format	Cover
☐ 1	Fashion.	Fashion design, referenced : a visual guide to the history, language & practice of fashion / Alicia Kennedy & Emily Banis Stoehrer with Jay Calderin.	2013	Book	
		Library Location: Main Collection Call Number: 746.92 K35f		Status: Available	
☐ 2	Fashion.	Advanced style / Ari Seth Cohen ; foreword by Maira Kalman ; interview by Dita von Teese.	2012	Book	
		Library Location: Main Collection Call Number: 746.92 C678a		Status: Available	
☐ 3	Fashion.	Ballgowns : British glamour since 1950 / Oriole Cullen, Sonnet Stanfill ; photographs by David Hughes.	2012	Book	
		Library Location: Main Collection Call Number: 746.920941 C967b		Status: Available	
☐ 4	Fashion.	Europe : rising fashion designers / Patrick Gottelier.	2012	Book	
		Library Location: Main Collection Call Number: 746.92094 G685e		Status: Available	
☐ 5	Fashion.	Meanings of dress.	2012	Book	
		Library Location: Reserve Collection 1st Floor Circulation Desk Call Number: 391.0019 M483m 2012		Status: Available	
☐ 6	Fashion.	Sartorialist : closer / Scott Schuman.	2012	Book	
		Library Location: Main Collection Call Number: 746.92 S392s 2012		Status: Available	
☐ 7	Fashion.	Steal her style : fashion icons and how to get their look / Sarah Kennedy.	2012	Book	
		Library Location: Main Collection Call Number: 746.92 K36s		Status: Available	

Just as there are numerous subject headings for Fashion, there are also numerous titles listed under each subject heading. These titles can also help you narrow your focus.

In just this preliminary investigation, we are presented with a variety of options for narrowing the initial subject. Perhaps you realize that you want to do research on fashion blogs or on one fashion blogger in particular and her or his influence on the fashion world. Or perhaps you'd like to talk about fashion jewelry and the new business models created by artisans on the East coast. You can even be so specific as to choose a specific piece of clothing or accessory to research, focusing on the accessory's early history or development: how about *boutonnieres*?

It can also be just as helpful to take a careful look inside the books that you find when trying to identify a topic for your research. If you would like to write about Mahatma Gandhi, for example, but are having a difficult time figuring out exactly what *about* him you would like to research, try inspecting the table of contents in a book to find a topic that interests you. *The Essential Gandhi: An Anthology of His Writing on His Life, Work, and Ideas* (New York: Vintage Press, 2002), for instance, has chapters that include the following in its second edition:

Civil Disobedience Succeeds
Gandhi's Road to Jail
Victory in South Africa
Segregation in India
Sex, Sanitation, and Segregation
Gandhi's Advice to Negroes
Gandhi on Socialism and Communism

If you see a chapter title that interests you, perhaps one of those listed, read the chapter more thoroughly and decide whether you would like to let one of these more specific subjects inform your research topic. Indexes are also good places to look, as the headings provided there will inspire many of the same ideas as will the table of contents.

Using Questions to Refine Your Topics

Once you have created a list of possible research topics, it is time to start working through your list to find the best option for your essay: what aspect of this topic can be argued appropriately within the span of the paper? How many resources and what kinds will I need to be able to make this argument effectively? Since research is often about inquiry, you can begin this process by raising these and additional questions about the topics in your list. These questions should push you to further define what *exactly* you want to say about the topics you have identified.

What kinds of questions should you ask? Well, that depends. You'll have a sense of whether you're asking the right questions once you have a workable topic and argument for your research paper. It's probably best to avoid the kinds of questions that lead to "yes" or "no" answers; rather, you're looking for questions whose answers speak to particular aspects of the topic.

Here are a few possibilities. While we can't provide you with an exact formula—a formula in this instance won't be helpful anyway—we can, however, model for you several possibilities that you can adapt to suit your own work.

Let's look at aspects of this process together, using the examples we've cited earlier in the chapter.

Using journalistic questions can help set boundaries for your topic: Who? When? Where? What? Why?
For example:

General subject:	Fashion
Who?	Women
When?	1960s
Where?	America
What?	Miniskirts
Why?	To express and empower

Possible Research Question

How did the miniskirt reflect not only the cultural movements of the 1960s but also the economic boom of that era?

Is your research aimed at a particular audience—in addition to the instructor?

If so, what might that audience want to know? For instance, are you writing to an advanced, highly expert group of film critics when you write about scary movies, or are you writing for a general, somewhat educated audience?

Possible Research Question for an Informed Audience

How do the cinematic techniques of Brian dePalma, particularly mise-en-scene and cross-cutting, parallel and pay homage to selected films of Alfred Hitchcock?

Another Example

How do aspects of Hitchcock's Psycho influence the films of Brian dePalma?

Possible Research Question for a General Audience

How well do scary movies do at the box office, and how does their economic performance often defy the reviews published by critics?

Ask yourself what you think the audience might already know.

What is common knowledge about the subject, and what might be aspects of the subject that you can bring to light? Consider the very large topic of World War II. Ask yourself, then, "What are things that the general public already knows about this subject? What's worth writing about?"

Things people know (or should) about World War II: Japanese bombing of Pearl Harbor in 1941; Axis Powers (Germany, Italy, Japan); Key Figures or Issues (Franklin D. Roosevelt, Winston Churchill, Adolf Hitler and Nazism).

Things people may not know (and you may come across these in pre-searching): Gender roles switching, with men away at war and women

40

out of the home and at work and in factories; specific effects of pivotal battles; the oppression of Jews, Gypsies, and homosexuals in Germany and elsewhere; Italian participation in the war; the days leading up to Pearl Harbor; the time after the European war had been won—but before the war in the Pacific was resolved.

However, there are aspects of the general knowledge topics that could—and should—be investigated as possibilities for research, as "general knowledge" sometimes refers to knowledge that merely scratches the surface of an issue. The point is that you should be aware of what your audience knows and what you might contribute to advancing the reader's awareness and knowledge of a subject.

Possible Research Question (or, in this case, topic)
Although many students learn in high school about the Holocaust, many might not be aware of attempts on the part of Jews to escape Germany on transports designed for both adults and children—some with success, some not—and the complicity of the United States in foiling one particular rescue attempt.

The subjects we've provided as an example here are, of course, just examples, and they are likely less than relevant to the work you need to do. The point, however, is this: the possibilities for research topics are boundless, and the challenge remains to narrow a topic and find a focus for your research efforts.

That is, it is essential to focus your thinking and move toward a research topic that is specific enough so that you can explore it within the time allowed and pages required for your essay. And, as we often tell our students, the more specific and manageable the topic is, the easier it will be to successfully write your research paper.

We encourage you to keep pushing for a narrower and more focused topic, continuously asking yourself the following:

- Does my topic still seem too broad?
- Could I do sufficient research on this subject within the time constraint of my assignment?

- Do I feel that I know where to begin my work, or do I feel over-whelmed by all of the information available on this topic? If so, how might I begin to sort through this information?

The answers to these questions should help you identify whether you are ready to move forward with the research process.

Turning Personal Interests Into Appropriate Research Topics

Often, when talking with students who are struggling to find something to write about, we find that they have overlooked something central: their personal experiences. While it is important to distinguish between personal writing and argument-focused, academic writing, it is also important that you begin to develop the capability to analyze your own interests and experiences in ways that are reflective of critical thinking.

Don't underestimate your own ability to turn your personal experiences into appropriate research topics. Consider your personal interests, your cultural heritage, and social issues that affect you and those around you. Any of these could lead to viable research topics—topics in which you will be particularly invested!

SAMPLE STUDENT RESEARCH TOPICS—SOME IN DISCIPLINES, SOME INTERDISCIPLINARY

Earth Sciences:	The increase of impermeable land in urban centers has increased instances of flooding. The effects of glacial deterioration on small coastal habitats in Alaska
Literature:	Women in the work of Aime Cesaire Economics and *Their Eyes Were Watching God*
History:	The evolution of the Chicago teachers' union The rise of tobacco and the American plantation *Uncle Tom's Cabin* and the end of slavery

Art History:	Pablo Picasso and political propaganda
	Gordon Parks and the democratizing of photography
Public Policy:	The deteriorating safety net for America's poor
	Nuclear nonproliferation in the twentieth century

Finding Significance and Identifying an Audience

One of the most important aspects of writing your research essay will be identifying and assessing your audience. For most students new to the research process, the concept of an audience can be a little confusing. Who is your primary audience, anyway? Are you writing this essay for your instructor? What about your classmates? Should you anticipate that a larger academic community will receive your work?

The truth is, it can be tricky to negotiate through these answers as a student writer. While you likely cannot expect for your work to be read by academics in the larger field of study, you do need to imagine an audience larger than just your instructor and your peers.

You see, writing a research essay is, in some ways, similar to having a conversation. The scope of your research will be greatly informed by whom you imagine having this conversation *with*—and the ways in which it is most appropriate to address that particular audience. For instance, is your audience highly educated? A good friend who's smart but who knows nothing of your subject? Experts in the field?

Think about the following questions:

- To whom am I writing?
- Who stands to benefit from the research I am doing?
- How can I insure that my audience is interested in my topic? How can I further define my essay's purpose to further pique their interest?
- How much can I assume my audience already knows about my topic?
- How can I demonstrate my authority on the subject?

43

The style, tone, and diction of your writing will be affected by these answers. You must determine who your audience is, and then you must find an approach best suited to that particular audience.

Diction and Tone

In addition to what you have read in Chapter 2, it is important to consider diction and tone. Your choice of language and your tone will (or should) have everything to do with assessing your audience appropriately and then understanding how best to address that audience.

For instance, here is a situation that emphasizes the importance of choosing your words (diction) carefully: if you are asked by your parent to wake up your young sibling—who has recently done something to annoy you—your choice of words and tone will likely differ than if your parent has asked you to wake up your kind (and generous) visiting aunt or uncle. And it's not unusual for us to have to code-switch (that is, change our language and word choice as would be right for a particular situation) from word choices and tone that are appropriately used among our friends to language and tone that are appropriately used in school or on the job.

While "CU LTR" might work well for a text message to friends and family, it likely will not work well in writing an academic paper where highly refined conventions apply. (It likely isn't the best way to text a supervisor or instructor, either.) Keep in mind the need to address your possibly complex audiences appropriately when you are writing.

Crafting a Thesis or Posing a Research Question

Once you have decided on a topic, you must begin mapping out your game plan for the rest of your research and the best way to argue your point of view. Usually, it is best to begin this process by articulating your topic as either a thesis statement or a research question. This statement or question—whichever best suits your particular focus—will be the guiding idea for the direction of your essay. Therefore, it is important that you identify what you will argue as soon as you are ready to begin your work. (And, of course, remember that "argument" in this context doesn't mean something combative; rather, it is a statement of what you expect to prove in your paper, a helpful guide for your reader—as well as for you.)

A thesis statement is something of a signpost. It condenses your essay's argument or intention into one or two sentences that usually, although not always, will appear within the first few paragraphs of your essay. The thesis will help you organize your ideas, and—if done correctly—it will help provide your reader with a signpost that explains what the essay will be about, what information you are trying to relay, and what argument you will be making. In most instances, a strong thesis statement is an expected and highly significant

45

component of a successful research paper. The absence of a thesis statement, or a poorly crafted one, can signify a lack of focus on the part of the writer.

A successful thesis statement will do the following:

- Give direction and focus to an essay or research paper. This direction assists both the writer (by serving as a tool for planning and organizing the essay) and the readers (by serving as a road map for the paper).
- Provide claims that will be backed by evidence throughout the body of the essay. Thesis statements are not statements of fact; you must support your assertions with accountable and credible research.
- Be narrow and concise. Remember, the scope of the essay's focus must fit the amount of time available to research and the number of pages required in the assignment. Again, don't confuse yourself and, ultimately, your readers, by announcing too broad a thesis.
- Engage your readers and allow them to see the purpose of your research.
- Preempt the possibility of your reader surveying your thesis statement and asking, "So what?" because of its clear purpose.

Some Examples:

Miniskirts are signs of empowerment. (Ineffective) The writer has not written a thesis that can be readily proved by evidence because the statement is too broad. Whose empowerment? The fashion industry? People wearing the miniskirt?

Are miniskirts appealing to men? (Ineffective) The writer has written a thesis statement that isn't a thesis statement—anything with a possible "yes" or "no" answer is not something that can be argued in a research paper.

While popular lore seems to indicate that women's hemlines rise and fall with the economy, recent history proves that fashion trends stem from far more complex economic contexts. (BETTER) This is a more restricted thesis statement and will be followed by another statement that indicates how the writer plans to prove his or her argument—indicating what are, in fact, the more complex economic contexts that will be explained.

Of course, while it is best to begin your research process by reviewing the sources you've gathered and then crafting a thesis statement, the statement itself should remain flexible until you have finished your essay. Throughout the research process, you may, and undoubtedly will, find new evidence that leads to a revision of your initial argument and that helps you reshape it.

The Difference between a Topic (or General Subject) and an Argument

To reiterate: Your *thesis* allows you to effectively *argue a point of view regarding your subject*, as the differences among the following will illustrate. Note how the writer narrows down the general subject toward an effective thesis that argues a point of view:

Topic/General Subject:	Pollution
Type of Pollution That Interests Me:	Water
Cause of This Pollution:	Oil Spills
Specific Example That Interests Me:	The BP Gulf Oil Spill

This particular student is interested in the effects of the oil spill on gulf beach resorts—in this instance, because the student grew up in this region, and family members' business interests were affected by the disaster. After studying and analyzing a wide range of sources on the economic impact of the Gulf Oil Spill, the student narrows the topic still further to analyze the economic comeback of the gulf region and develops the following working thesis/argument:

> *While British Petroleum has committed funds and other resources to the redevelopment of affected resorts in the Gulf region, the efficacy of these efforts remains under dispute.*
>
> *The rebuilding of Gulf Coast tourism is the result not only of the passage of time but also of strategic efforts and partnerships among industry, small business owners, and marketers.*

What is effective about this thesis statement and the argument it puts forth? The precise meaning of the arguments is very clear. In the first, for instance, the writer has promised to explain the nature of the dispute and the arguments for and against the effectiveness of the efforts made by the oil company to rectify a difficult situation. It is also strongly suggested that the writer will provide just enough context for the intelligent reader so that the reader has a basis for judging the arguments.

Here is another example of a complex thesis within a paragraph that points to the writer's argument. The student, Nadezh Mayo, writes about "Sexuality, Race, and Class in the Court Case *Rhinelander v. Rhinelander*"[1]:

> This particular case seems to have disappeared from popular accounts of history. It was not a Supreme Court case and it is not as well known as other cases pertaining to racial restrictions on marriage (in fact, only two lawyers are known to have access to the full court transcripts [Onwuachi-Willig, 2401]). For example, many

---

[1] The full text of Ms. Mayo's research paper appears in the Appendix.

48

people have heard of the case *Loving v. Virginia*, in which an inter-racial couple from Virginia fought for the right to be together in 1967 and won, legalizing interracial marriage throughout the United States. The case of *Rhinelander v. Rhinelander* may not be as well known, but the trial is an equally important snapshot in American history. The court proceedings express American conceptions of race in the 1920s, as well as American ideas about the roles of men, women, and sexual boundaries in the context of race. To describe the trial as an attack on interracial marriage and the "pollution" of the white race by blacks is not wrong, but it is incomplete. Upon closer examination, the court case *Rhinelander v. Rhinelander*, although fought on the grounds of racial fraud, in fact has as much to do with sexuality and gender as it does with race. Indeed, it is nearly impossible to think about the *Rhinelander* case without addressing the important interactions of race, sexuality, and class in public perceptions of Alice—a poor, black woman.

As Mayo's purpose is complex, her thesis is not neatly boiled down into one, simple sentence; rather, it takes several well-crafted sentences to make clear what she will argue.

Ideas Into Practice

As we have discussed in this chapter, developing a research question involves working through a series of steps, beginning with identifying broad subjects that interest you. Use the chart we have provided here as a guide to help you keep track of your topic ideas and to organize the notes you collect during the pre-searching process. Keep in mind that research itself is somewhat recursive. That is, you likely will find yourself doing the types of evaluation of sources that we suggest in the following chapter as you gather the resources you need to help you focus your paper—as we delineated in this chapter.

General Subject:

Pre-searching Notes:

What Interests You Most:

Narrowed Topic:

Thesis or Research Question:

CHAPTER five

The Wikipedia Problem: Evaluating and Trusting Sources in a Digital Age

talking points

- Why is it important that I find credible resources?
- What makes a resource reliable?
- How can I evaluate resources?
- Why do I have to go to the library when I have Google?
- You mean I can't get all of my information from Wikipedia?

In 1998, Google's search engine went live. Three years later, in 2001, Wikipedia debuted as the first online collaborative encyclopedia. While we are quick to think of both of these Internet start-ups as cultural boons, it's also important to consider the ways that both Google and Wikipedia have in some ways been a detriment to our intellectual lives.

> *Quick Fact*
> *"Google" was first used as a verb in 1998—the same year the site debuted. It was added to the Oxford English Dictionary in 2006.*

Research in a Digital Age
Digital Information: A Detriment or a Boon?

Most likely, you don't remember a time when you couldn't quickly find the answers to all of your questions through an Internet search. You've been part of a world where you can access an inordinate amount of information without having to consult anything in hard copy, much less a book. In many ways, you're part of a population that has more easy access to more information than ever before.

Is this a good thing? Well, that depends. Having more information than one can process argues for careful analysis and evaluation of these sources. And that need seems more acute now than ever. We've only begun realizing how this accessibility—this "instant answer culture"—has changed the ways that many students engage in academic practices. In particular, the way you conduct research and the way you think about research have inarguably been altered by these digital worlds.

But some things don't change: that is, good research takes time, and, while information may be easier to access in a digital era, the scholarly processes necessary to produce credible and valuable academic writing haven't changed much at all. In fact, the ability to discern the quality and appropriateness of information is more necessary than ever.

So, while we as professors want our students to develop a technological literacy that enables them to make use of the wealth of digital content available to them, we also want students to understand the importance of honoring a long-standing tradition of scholarly research, one that transcends the medium (digital, book, etc.) holding the information you need.

However, among any concern about the need for the enhanced ability to sift through information, there's additional good news. You are more technologically savvy than any other generation. And, as much as we want you to be able to thoughtfully navigate your way through this sea of information, the truth remains: In many ways, that access presents endless possibilities for scholarly research and academic engagement—but with many resulting challenges. You have opportunities and readily accessible information in ways that were unforeseen even a few years ago; we want to help you assess and use these in as savvy and in as critically a way as possible.

Scuba Diving versus Jet Skiing

To reiterate: In 2008, *The Atlantic* published Nicholas Carr's "Is Google Making Us Stupid?," in which the author argues that our frequent use of the Internet is causing physiological changes to our brains. Clearly, this potentially has great impact on the way we read and engage with texts. The piece seemed to strike a chord, quickly becoming popular. In explaining how his own reading habits and abilities have altered noticeably, Carr notes, "Once I was a scuba diver in the sea of words. Now I zip along the surface like a guy on a jet ski."

We have seen this metaphor play out in the way many students engage—or in the way they *aren't* engaging—with sources in their academic writing. More and more, students are doing the kind of skimming Carr alludes to in his article. Students pull quotes from sources to satisfy a minimum number of resources in the bibliography, and they aren't thoroughly evaluating and reading the sources from which they are quoting. Do you recognize yourself here?

We want you to be mindful of this phenomenon when conducting your research: the ways frequent Internet use may have an impact on your ability to engage with and fully understand and analyze texts. Constantly ask yourself, "Am I scuba diving or am I jet skiing?"

Evaluating Sources

Why Do I Need to Trust Sources, Anyway?

Trustworthy sources, and your acknowledgment of those sources, contribute to your being a trustworthy writer. No matter the source or topic, an expectation among writers—academic or otherwise—is that you are accountable, that is, that you can be counted on as a writer who has done the often painstaking homework of finding the right information to back up your point of view. Remember, these factors can go a long way toward demonstrating your ethos as a research writer.

It is generally expected that you are arguing a point fairly and accurately, that you are arguing it in your own words, and that you have consulted appropriate sources that back up your argument. Equally important is that you have acknowledged those sources as having contributed to your own work. Just as good writing takes time, so, too, does finding and analyzing the right sources for your work—as does using them appropriately.

Easier Isn't Always Better

All that said, the heading for this section, and what follows, might seem obvious: Not all resources are created equal. That is, one of your primary tasks as a researcher is to determine which resources are reliable and which are not so that you can craft that accountable, well-defended argument. That said, this task was considerably easier before the Internet came along. Before the availability of search engines and online databases, researchers relied on card catalogs and large machines displaying microfiche copies of newspapers and other types of printed, archived materials. The smart researcher-writer spent hours perusing library bookshelves, reading through potential resources, and thumbing through printed indexes, often waiting weeks for books through interlibrary loan services. (And despite the Internet, the latter is still true.)

While digitalized searches have made it easier for researchers to find and fully use such resources, the Internet has also made it more difficult to discern whether those sources are dependable, as virtually anyone can create and launch a website and make it seem authoritative. To reiterate, here's the thing about websites: anybody can have one. The Internet has made it possible for large amounts of often unfiltered information to be shared in effortless fashion; it has also made it possible for people to "publish" their work—work that, oftentimes, hasn't been reviewed or fact-checked by anyone, much less a responsible and reputable editor. It's true that you can access scholarly databases, government reports, and other valuable resources online, but you have to be savvy in the way you search for and decide to use these sources.

Think about your recent Internet searches. If, for example, you are using the keywords "fast food" to search for resources to use in an essay about America's obesity epidemic, you are as likely to stumble upon a website entitled *Bob's Burger Adventures* as you are to find a comprehensive study of fast food nutrition from the United States Government.

It is likely that the first source in the Google list will be a sponsored source, not necessarily one that's appropriate for your research project. Perhaps the first link is the result of a concerted effort by the site's owner or author to "game" the Google system and ensure that the site appears as a top link. (You are likely aware that the top links aren't necessarily the most authoritative sources on a given topic—and yet it might be. It's up to you to determine this.) As a researcher, then, know that it is your job to evaluate whether these sources meet your needs and meet the standards of the academic communities in which you are participating—and those for whom you are often writing.

Whereas the Internet presents a wide variety of information with an equally unpredictable range of quality and reliability, libraries (apart from access to the Internet in library buildings) present a different set of opportunities. In a library, you are surrounded by texts and materials that have—in one way or another—been vetted. That is, books have gone through long and tedious publication processes involving initial review by a potential publisher, reviews by other scholars in the field, and rounds of revision—and all this before publication. Then, many books will have been reviewed in significant journals after publication. Similarly, magazine and newspaper articles have often been fact-checked by multiple staffers, and scholarly publications in most journals also have been peer reviewed.

So, while the Internet certainly does house valuable information, it is necessary that you hold Web-based resources particularly accountable for the same level of credibility that you would find—perhaps more easily and reliably—on library shelves.

The Good News: Using Wikipedia and Google Effectively

Despite what we have said about how the Internet requires us to be more discerning researchers, the truth remains that at some point in the process, most researchers will take to the Web. It is in acknowledging these realties—and acknowledging the ways in which our intellectual lives now often inhabit digital spaces—that we want to find a happy medium. That is, just as we would not encourage you to do all of your research on Wikipedia or Google, we also do not want to discourage you from approaching these valuable resources in smart and savvy ways.

The truth is that both Wikipedia and Google *can* be valuable tools during the research process. Of course, you likely use these websites to conduct your own casual "research" every single day. You Google reviews of the Thai restaurants in your area. You look up movie times. You find a reliable hair stylist. You quickly scan the Wikipedia entry about a famous philosopher that a friend mentioned in passing. We all do these things; we are all conducting some form of research—using these online tools—regularly.

When it comes to academic research, however, it is necessary that we approach these Web resources differently. Let's discuss some ways to do that.

Google

Google, as we discussed earlier in the chapter, is one of the world's most popular search engines. As you already know, using Google gives you access to more information than could ever be quantified. That said, the results you get in Google are completely dependent on the way you execute your search—and on the ways in which you evaluate the results for their usefulness and credibility. Later on in this book, we will talk about using effective keywords and Boolean phrases that will assist your search. However, there are steps you can take, even before you enter your keywords, to ensure that you are targeting your search to yield the most credible and appropriate results.

There are two tips that are especially helpful. The first is to try your searches using Google Scholar. Executing a search on Google is like asking the engine to rummage through a series of a million drawers, looking for anything—reviews, photographs, websites—that has the keywords you typed into the search bar. Using Google Scholar (scholar.google.com), then, is like telling the search engine to look only in drawers containing academic sources. That is, when you do a search using Google Scholar, all of your results should come from reputable scholarly publications. So you are much more likely to find the kind of information you will need for your research projects.

Another way to refine the search is to limit the results to websites ending in .edu, .org, or .gov. These domains—the websites ending with these suffixes—are much more likely to provide researchers with high-quality information than are many websites ending in .com or .net. You can refine your searches in this way by accessing the "Advanced Settings" on your Google homepage.

Wikipedia

Just as you can approach Google searches in a sophisticated way, there are also ways that you can use Wikipedia to your advantage. While most academic researchers likely would not use Wikipedia articles in their work, as they are user created and not always fact checked, many Wikipedia entries now contain something that can be very valuable during the research process: a bibliography.

If you scroll to the bottom of nearly any entry on Wikipedia, you will find a list of sources—and many of those lists include hyperlinks. This means several things: not only are the authors of the various Wikipedia entries telling you where they found the information they used to write the article, but they are also, in many cases, linking you directly to that information somewhere else on the Internet. So, while you wouldn't want to use Wikipedia as an exclusive resource in your own work, you can use Wikipedia to find other resources—many that would, after you examine them, be considered valuable and credible. This kind of "bibliographical diving," as we like to call it, can be extremely fruitful, leading to a trail of resources—many of which might have their own bibliographies, too!

Therefore, there are myriad ways to use the Internet's limitless collection of resources to your advantage. Remember that you have control of how you navigate this sea of information, that you are responsible for determining the validity of that information, and that there are ways to ensure that what you find along the way will be useful to you as you begin doing your own writing.

Although we speak specifically about Google and Wikipedia because of their preeminence as this book is written, the larger point is independent of the particular resource that you are using. No matter what source you use, approach it with thought and careful analysis, intellectual qualities that transcend the medium or the website.

Determining Appropriate Resources

Before you can begin assessing the credibility of resources, you first need to determine what kinds of resources will be the most useful to you. What kind of essay are you writing? What is the topic? And—more important—what is the purpose of your essay? Do you want to share new information? Present an opinion? Make an informed argument? Does your information need to be qualitative or quantitative or both? (see Table 5.1)

Table 5.1   TYPES OF DATA

As you move forward with your research, what kinds of data will best help you support your arguments?

QUALITATIVE DATA	QUANTITATIVE DATA
Qualitative (quality) data are based on observation, description, and other immeasurable information.	Quantitative (quantity) data deal with numbers, statistics, and information that can be measured.

Answering these questions before you begin looking for resources will help your search stay goal-oriented. Knowing what kind of resources you *don't* need can be as useful as knowing what kind of resources you do need.

Scholarly versus Popular Sources

Chances are (again, depending on your topic) that you will likely make use of both scholarly and popular resources. Scholarly resources, such as research-based books and articles published in academic journals, are often written for an audience of faculty members—that is, scholars and researchers. These include publications such as *African Studies Quarterly*, the *Journal of Religious and Popular Culture*, and *The American Journal of Medicine*. As we mentioned earlier, most scholarly resources have been through a peer-review process. Most often, they will also include citations, footnotes, and a bibliography.

Popular resources, on the other hand, are written for a more general audience. Many of these are the kinds of publications you would find while standing in line at the grocery store. However, it is important to understand that credibility varies even among popular resources. *Time* magazine and *Newsweek*, for instance, are both very reputable newsmagazines, with credible reporters and commentators.

However, magazines such as *US Weekly* and *People*—while culturally relevant—are not nearly as likely to offer the kind of reliable information you need when writing academically, unless, of course, your assignment is a critical analysis of these types of publications. Even then, however, you will likely seek other reviewers and critics of popular culture as you delineate your arguments and work to support them.

The Art of Skimming

Having just maligned the scuba diving/jet ski simile, we do, nonetheless, encourage you to learn the art of looking through various sets of materials thoroughly, effectively—and yet efficiently. This is where appropriate skimming—as opposed to the shallow knowledge that

Nicholas Carr warns against—can be useful, especially when you first begin reviewing materials. It will be necessary to learn ways to judge fairly quickly whether a source will be worth your careful perusal and study. This is when you might want to use strategies known as "pre-reading," such as looking carefully at the Table of Contents; looking carefully at the index; the overall structure of longer books and articles; and, for academic articles, taking time to study the abstract rather than the entire piece (at least at the start).

Learning to "read" these various components of (especially) longer sources can assist in your sorting through overwhelming amounts of materials in a responsible way. For instance, in a collection of articles and longer texts, your review might result in your using only one chapter out of, say, twenty. Don't discount longer volumes or texts as you evaluate resources; parts of a source might prove to be very useful to you later on. Cultivating the art of skimming, or, one might say, "selective looking," might help.

Evaluating All Sources

While you need to be especially careful when looking for resources on the Internet, you should also be asking yourself a series of questions that test the reliability of any resource you find—whether online or in print. These questions can help you begin to analyze and screen sources and determine their credibility—and, ultimately, their usefulness to you and to your work.

Some Questions to Ask When Evaluating Resources

What do you know about the author?

For most of the types of writing that you will do at a college or university, it is important that you know as much as possible about the person who authored your source. In scholarly publications, for instance, you will always see both the author's name and the author's academic affiliation. Is the author associated with a university or professional organization? What is the author's educational background? Is the author considered an expert in his or her field? Is the author in any way self-interested, or trying to sell something, that might undermine his or her credibility? The more you know about the person that created the text, the more you can trust that the text will be a reliable resource for your research.

At the same time, however, you may want to determine and analyze what others in the field think about a particular author. For instance, someone with what appear to be good academic credentials might, for instance (and in an especially extreme example), prove to be a denier of historical fact.

Is the source backed by a reputable publisher?

With printed texts and materials, it is usually easy to determine who published a given work. You can find this information on the copyright page or the spine of a book. Who, then, is the publisher? Have you heard of this publishing company before? What other work have they published? University presses are usually highly regarded, and the books they publish have undergone an especially rigorous process of evaluation.

Of course, just as someone can publish his or her own website and make it seem authoritative, writers can also self-publish their own books through corporations that take otherwise unpublishable manuscripts (by most standards) and publish them for a price, usually paid for by the author. So, while a printed text may seem reliable, it may not have been vetted by reviewers or editors before being allowed into print.

The point? Be judicious when evaluating all resources—even hard copy books—so that sources on which you rely to bolster or to advance your argument are credible. To a great extent, your own credibility as a writer depends on these choices.

Again, the issue of credibility is exacerbated with online sources. With online sources, you must also make sure that information is sponsored by a well-known university or organization—that it has been evaluated appropriately. Much as you can look at the copyright page in a book for information, you can also look at the URL of an online source. Web addresses that end in .gov and .edu, for instance, can *generally* be trusted.

Has the source been peer reviewed?

As we have noted, most published academic writing—whether an article or a book—has gone through a peer-review process. Through peer review, experts in the respective field read through and respond to written scholarship or the results of research. For that piece of writing to be published, these peer reviewers will have first acknowledged that the author has made a credible and significant contribution to the field.

You will find that comparatively few popular magazines, newspapers, or online resources have been through similar review processes, and, depending on the topic and the purpose of your own writing, you will want to use the latter type of source very carefully and wisely.

Is the source current? Does it need to be?

There are times when it is important to look at older, often archival, research as a way to make your point and support your argument. As always, these considerations will depend on your topic and the purpose of your writing. For instance, in an argument one of us advanced regarding scholarly work in a particular field, it was important to look at articles in journals dating from the mid-1950s to illustrate that many of our contemporary concerns are not, in fact, new. If you are a history major writing a senior thesis on the Civil War, and depending on your topic, you might also choose to dig into documents and sources from the time of that conflict. A literature major might also find that documents related to popular culture or reviews at the time a particular work was written will be useful for his or her analysis of, say, a previously ignored novel.

Yet for many writing assignments, however, you must be aware that information is always changing and—if the topic demands it and you want your academic writing to be relevant and timely—you need to make sure that your resources are also contemporary. What is the publication date? Is there a newer edition of a particular source? Are there more contemporary voices that you should consult? Part of your analytical and decision-making process as you select the sources to support your writing might be to determine whether your resources are current, and if they are older, to understand why you have made a careful and deliberate choice to use them. Is it a seminal work in the field? Have there been critiques of the book, but critiques that do not dispute the basic premise—or, depending on your topic, sources that legitimately dispute the basic premise of an older work?

Does the source provide bibliographical data?

In most instances, you will be required to create a bibliography when writing a research paper. It is important that you are able to communicate—through citations and footnotes—where you found the information you have chosen to use as support for your argument. So it makes sense that the best kinds of resources are often the ones that are equally accountable for where their information came from, too. Look for sources that have bibliographies so that you can analyze what types of work the author used to support the central arguments of the article or book.

Has this source been cited by other writers?

One of the best ways to tell whether you can trust a source is by figuring out whether other scholars have read and trusted that same source as well. You can use databases, such as the *MLA International Bibliography*, to see whether other scholars have cited the source that you are considering using in your own work. And even Google offers opportunities to research how often a scholarly article has been cited by other scholars.

All that said, be aware, though, that there are many articles that—for one reason or another—never quite catch on in the scholarly world but that are equally worthy of your consideration as you research your subject and topic. Sometimes you might find a highly credible scholarly gem that others have missed. Such are the pleasures and challenges of being an accountable researcher and writer.

Is the argument reasonable?

Although the degree to which a resource is being reasonable is highly subjective, trust that you are savvy enough to know whether a source is being fair and trustworthy. Most reputable scholars will do their best to present all sides of an argument, and they will not intentionally present a biased point of view. Be wary of sources that seem aggressively opinionated and one sided—again, depending on your topic.

CARS: Credibility, Accuracy, Reasonableness, Support

Using CARS is an effective tool to use for evaluating resources. This set of criteria will help you as you assess the quality of the sources you find (see Table 5.2).

Table 5.2   CARS

The CARS rubric is yet another way to determine the quality of your information.

Credibility	Trustworthy source, author identified, can be contacted, known or respected authority, author's credentials, evidence of quality control, organizational support.
Accuracy	Current, date of update/revision, factual, detailed, exact, comprehensive, audience and purpose reflect intentions of completeness and accuracy, gives the whole truth.
Reasonableness	Fair, balanced, objective, reasoned, no conflict of interest, absence of fallacies or slanted tone. Is the information likely, possible, or probable?
Support	Listed sources, contact information, available corroboration, claims supported, documentation supplied. A source you can triangulate (find at least two other sources that support it).

*http://nurseweb.ucsf.edu/www/a1_p4v2.html

No matter how masterful we may be as writers, we are only as good as the evidence we use to advance our arguments. As an intellectual thinker, your ability to find, analyze, and best use appropriate sources enhances your accountability and your ethos as a communicator.

Ideas Into Practice

This checklist is to help you capture what is sometimes the "randomness" of finding good sources—in other words, "things I found as I was looking for something else." We suggest that you make a few copies of this checklist and keep it with you as you begin your research. Try using the comments section to document any information or ideas you may have about the sources you find. Keeping organized notes throughout the research process will also help to better organize your ideas once you begin writing.

EVALUATING RESOURCES ➤ A Checklist

The Source

Title: _____

Print or Web Resource: _____

Author: _____

Publisher: _____

Publication Date: _____

Author and Authority

Is the author credible?   Yes   No   Don't Know

Comment: _____

Is the source backed by a reputable
  publisher?   Yes   No   Don't Know

Comment: _____

Has the source been peer reviewed?　　Yes　No　Don't Know

Comment: _____

Does the source have a bibliography?　Yes　No　Don't Know

Comment: _____

Response and Reason

Has the author's work been well received
　　by peers?　　　　　　　　　　　　Yes　No　Don't Know

Comment: _____

Has this source been cited by other
　　reputable scholars?　　　　　　　　Yes　No　Don't Know

Comment: _____

Does the author's argument seem fair
　　and balanced?　　　　　　　　　　Yes　No　Don't Know

Comment: _____

CHAPTER **six**

What Counts and Why? Finding and Engaging Sources

talking points

- How do I find resources?
- What's the difference between a search engine and an online database?
- How do I navigate all of the resources in the library?
- Do keywords make a difference in search results?
- What's the difference between a primary and secondary resource—and why does it matter?

At this point, you should have a narrowed research topic in mind. Although you have probably done a bit of pre-searching (as we encouraged in Chapter 4), it's likely that you have yet to find all of the resources that you will use to write your essay. In this chapter, we will help you begin that process.

Finding Resources

Of course, the best way to begin to find resources is to first identify the kinds of resources that you will need. To start, think about what your instructor has asked of you. Do you have to have a specific number of resources or types of resources that you must find? Are online sources acceptable? Have you been discouraged from using any type of encyclopedia? Do your sources have to be peer reviewed—that is, with information published only after other professionals in the field have vetted it first? Take stock of your "must haves," and let them guide you through your research process.

You also need to think about your research topic and your essay's audience—both of which should inform the kinds of resources that you think will best support your argument. Does the nature of your argument lend itself to more popular resources, for instance, blogs and magazines? Or does your research question demand reputable and vetted sources, such as scholarly articles? The answers to questions such as these will influence the direction your research should take. Spend a little time developing a game plan before you hit the stacks, both virtual and brick and mortar.

Here are some basic research tips to help you get started:

Document Everything:
In a previous chapter, we talked about the importance of note taking. It is imperative that you keep track of information as you find it. You may find an article or a book now and decided that you don't want to use it, only to later find that it might have helped you. (And no matter how good your memory, it is best to assume that you won't remember that terrific source later on without writing it down or making a record of it in some other fashion.)

So start a working bibliography on day one, using note cards, the notes feature on your smartphone, a tablet, or a website (easybib.com, for example) to easily track the titles and authors of the sources as you find them. As you keep track of everything you find, you then have notes to direct you later in the research process, with your options for which sources to use at the maximum. And keep in mind that most online databases will also give you the option to e-mail yourself a link to the full article so that you can consult it later.

Collect Now, Sort Later:
The first few days spent researching can prove to be overwhelming. Depending on your topic, you will likely encounter an endless trail of resources—many more than you could ever reasonably use. Don't get bogged down with heavy reading just yet. It's perfectly acceptable to amass a pretty sizable collection of books, articles, and other materials that may—or may not—prove to be useful. Evaluate the resources quickly and efficiently (using the criteria we gave you in Chapter 5), and then plan to thumb through them more thoroughly later on. Again, having options is the key.

Don't Limit Yourself:
Yes, you will probably be able to find some interesting and relevant books in your school's library. However, you may also be able to find appropriate resources elsewhere: in a database of newspaper articles, in a scholarly journal, or even on a webcast. The point is this: the more avenues you exhaust, the more likely you are to find a diverse and varied array of resources that can, and will, add to your credibility as a researcher and provide options for the way you ultimately "slant" your argument and your work.

Knowing the Difference: Primary, Secondary, and Tertiary Sources

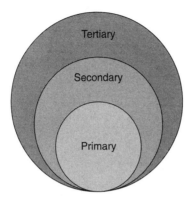

Although your sources are of various types, they are all interconnected.

As a researcher, you will likely be relying on a variety of sources to help you construct your argument. During the research process, you will come across three different types of resources: primary, secondary, and tertiary (see Table 6.1).

Primary sources are original materials. They are often firsthand accounts written or recorded by an eyewitness and may also contain raw data. Primary sources are "pure," without interpretation, and they have not been changed. Some examples of primary sources include photographs, patents, speeches, audio recordings of events, interviews, diaries, physical artifacts (fossils, historical clothing, etc.), letters, legal documents (birth certificate, marriage license, trial transcripts).

Secondary sources are more difficult to define. They are often created with the use of primary sources, and they may be the result of

71

someone having evaluated and interpreted raw data. So, while a primary source may be considered evidence, a secondary source is the result of reviewing and discussing that evidence. Some examples of secondary sources include biographies, scholarly writing (peer-reviewed articles and journals), reviews and critiques, dictionaries, and most magazine and newspaper articles.

Table 6.1   EXAMPLES OF PRIMARY, SECONDARY, AND TERTIARY SOURCES

TOPIC	PRIMARY	SECONDARY	TERTIARY
Horror films	Hitchcock's *The Birds*	Scholarly critics writing about the film; reviews of the film	*Encyclopedia of American Horror Films*
The civil rights movement	Transcripts of speeches by Martin Luther King, Jr.	Biography of Martin Luther King, Jr.	Wikipedia blurb about the civil rights movement
Fine art	Painting by Frida Kahlo	Review of painting by a reputable art critic	ArtStor database

Tertiary sources present a list or collection of primary and secondary sources. These sources are often seen as a guide to primary and secondary resources, as tertiary sources are presented as an overview. Keep in mind that most instructors (and those who adhere to their subject area conventions) will frown on tertiary sources as part of your bibliography—unless, of course, you're doing a study, say, of Wikipedia itself. Some examples of tertiary sources include manuals, indexes, databases, bibliographies, most textbooks, encyclopedias.

Finding Sources Online

Many, if not most, of the preliminary searches you will conduct as you begin the research process will take place on the Internet. Online search engines and databases are all readily accessible and are integral tools throughout your research process. However, knowing how to navigate these online tools efficiently and accurately can determine whether the results will help you with your research writing or confuse you even further.

This is why, and as we discussed in "The Wikipedia Problem," it is extremely important that you are able to evaluate and filter the information that you come across when using the Internet to find sources. Again, you have read a good deal about this in Chapter 5, and it is important that you keep the tips we gave you in mind—tips for conducting research in a digital age and for evaluating the resources you find. Use these tips to help you refine your evaluation skills.

Online Library Databases versus Internet Search Engines

When conducting research online, you can consult both your library's online database and more popular Internet search engines, such as Google and Yahoo.

The *online databases* for your school or local library provide access to sources that are, for the most part, more credible than others a researcher might find. Most libraries subscribe to a variety of academic and discipline-specific databases, giving you access to scholarly articles, newspapers, and magazines. So, when you search the library's database, the results will be limited to materials that have likely appeared in print and have previously gone through an editorial process.

Library databases, such as EBSCO, Academic Search Premier, JSTOR, and InfoTrac, are not often free and available to the public. You pay for access to these resources with your tuition dollars, and your school libraries will select databases that best serve the programs and classes that their respective institutions offer, increasing the likelihood that the resources you find through library databases will apply to the kinds of research you are asked to do in your class.

On the other hand, *Internet search engines*, as we've discussed earlier, provide access to a sea of information (or, depending on what you find, misinformation). Unlike library databases, however, the Internet has no gatekeeper. There aren't necessarily any librarians carefully selecting which resources should be available to you, any editors overseeing the various stages of publication, or any academics vetting and peer-reviewing the information you find.

So, whereas your database searches will almost certainly lead you to information that is organized and reliable, the information you find on the Internet will vary significantly in terms of quality. (Remember our earlier reference to *"Bob's Burger Adventures"*?) When using search engines, you have to be the most discerning about which sources are appropriate and which are not.

All this doesn't mean, of course, that these search engines can't provide you with useful resources. You just have to be savvy in your approach to both the language you use to conduct the search and the results provided (see Table 6.2).

Table 6.2   TOOLS FOR ONLINE RESEARCH

While both search engines and library databases can be useful to researchers, there are marked differences between the two.

SEARCH ENGINES	DATABASES
Free to the public	Paid for by your library
No gatekeeper	Content has been reviewed by librarians
Information is not always reliable	Resources have been through an editorial process
Information is disorganized	

Choosing Your Keywords Carefully

Whether using an online database or an Internet search engine, the keywords you use to execute your search will determine the quality of results that are returned to you.

> *Quick Fact*
> *The Library of Congress, which was established in 1800, consisted of 740 books and three maps. Today, the library houses more than 32 million titles and is the largest book collection in North America.*

A library database is nothing like Google. While it is acceptable to type in "scary movies" in Google, there are certain protocols for using library databases. For instance, the Library of Congress database archives resources about movies under the subject heading "film." So, if you type in "movies," you may not get the results that you want or need.

How can you get to know these keywords? The online "call page" for every resource will list not only the author and the title for each source, but it will also give the Library of Congress subject heading. Once you have identified one source that fits the scope of your project, you can then look to the call page for that source and find the subject heading that will lead you to further sources—because you have found the correct "keyword." However, even though Google sources might seem more forgiving, as you will always receive *some* type of result when you attempt to search through Google, you must still be very discriminating about what it is that you find.

Let's say, for example, that you want to do research on the overconsumption of fast food in America—a topic we have used as an example before. Your first instinct may be to open up Google and search for "McDonald's." Why not? McDonald's is the most popular fast food restaurant in the country, right? However, this search is likely to turn up a vast and overwhelming diverse network of information: addresses for the McDonald's nearest to you, nutritional information for the Big Mac and the double cheeseburger, photographs of hamburger packaging, reviews of local McDonald's restaurants, and so forth. Because there is so much information—often too much—identifying which information is appropriate and reliable can be a difficult and somewhat daunting task.

Instead, when you are conducting searches through any search engine, we encourage you to think carefully about the keywords or terms you use for your search. Here is another way to think about it: the larger the network of information you are tapping into, the more carefully you need to choose the keywords that you use to increase the likelihood that you will find what you're looking for.

While popular search engine results are not vetted or restricted by any particular parameters, the situation is different for your library's online databases, such as EBSCO, Academic Search Premiere, and so on, which are primarily limited to magazines, scholarly journals, and newspaper articles.

Let's take a look at the difference.

Here are the results when we search for "McDonald's" using Google's search engine:

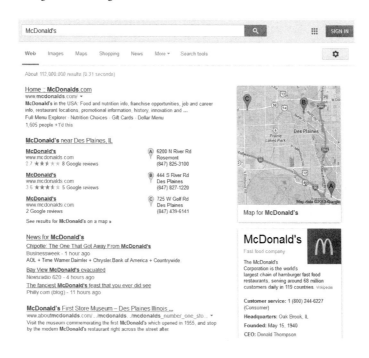

And here is what we get when we search for "McDonald's" as a keyword using EBSCO:

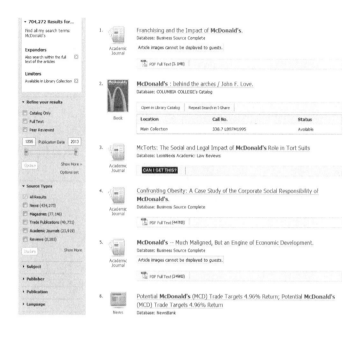

As you can see, the results vary enormously, and you need to target carefully the type of results you want. However, if neither of these yields the specific kind of information you seek, you will need to rethink your strategy. In other words, these search results serve as a good indication that your keyword or keywords need to be refined.

Boolean Searches

Boolean searches use the connecting words (called operators) "and," "or," or "not" to make your search phrases more specific. Using this type of phrasing when searching either popular Internet websites or library databases can help yield results that are more appropriate to your topic.

For example, searching for "McDonald's and obesity" will be much more fruitful to you than simply typing in "McDonald's."

In addition, Boolean searches limit the results to more specifically fit the scope of your search. If you just searched for "video games," for example, you will likely get thousands of results. If you search for "video games and violence," however, your results will be significantly refined, leaving you hundreds of options to sort through instead of thousands.

So, as we have mentioned many times in this chapter, the keywords you use to execute a search will most certainly determine how useful the results will be.

Finding Sources in the Library

While your first instinct might be to run to your laptop and begin searching for resources using your favorite search engine, we urge you to first make use of your college and local libraries. Remember what we've said before: libraries host collections of sources that have already been vetted, for the most part. Your chances of finding credible and reliable sources in your school library are much higher than your chances of finding them independently on the Internet.

Consequently, do resist the urge to do all of your research from the comfort of your own desk chair. And remember the pleasures of finding things that you happened to run across on your way to looking for something else. While this can happen online, it can also happen as you scan shelves of books or look through old microfiche screens.

Getting to know your library—and your library's online catalog—is half of the battle. And, luckily, some of that type of work actually *can* be done from your desk chair. Nearly all libraries, especially those associated with colleges and universities, have websites that are easily navigated.

For example, let's look at the library homepage for each of our institutions:

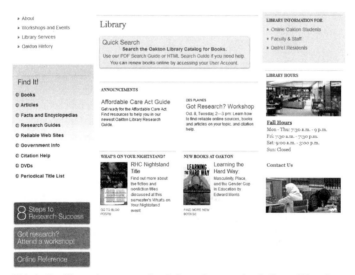

This is the library homepage for Oakton Community College. What information seems most important? What are similarities and differences with the pages at your own college?

And this is the library home page for Columbia College Chicago. What information seems most important? What are similarities and differences with the pages at your own college?

While the graphics, design, and layout among institutional websites may be significantly different, you will notice, however, that both websites offer similar options to students. Most notably, the homepages for both libraries provide immediate access to their online catalogs and databases.

Most likely, the homepage for your library will look very similar, and it will be useful for you to compare yours with these to see differences, similarities, and whether ways to find different types of information vary from institution to institution. As you look at these pages and investigate those at your institution, you will also have the option to search for a variety of texts, including books, articles, and multimedia materials.

Using Online Catalogs to Find Books

Your library's online catalog will help you search for books housed within the library by a variety of criteria: subject, author, keywords, title, and so forth. The catalog's chief function is to assist you in identifying the books that best meet the criteria you specified and then to direct you to where those books are located within the library.

As you can see, the first half of your work can be done online, but you may find that you will have to venture into the library to complete your search—and, we trust, that you will benefit from scanning shelves of books that might well turn up other possibilities for your work.

Find Books

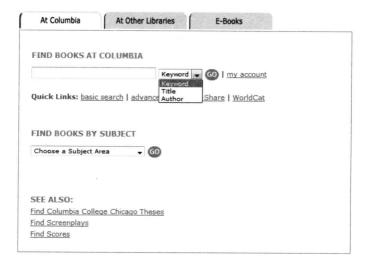

Columbia College Chicago. Most online card catalogs will resemble this one.

As you'll see in the graphics provided, the library homepages for both Oakton Community College and Columbia College Chicago provide students with quick and easy access to the card catalog. Look for the "Books" or "Library Catalog" link, and there is where you will begin your search.

Since you likely have some experience navigating library catalogs, we are not going to walk through the step-by-step process of initiating these searches. Once you've found any number of books, articles, and the like—and once these are recorded in writing or some other way of documenting the source information (yes, even phone photos of the title page of a book and its call number and other relevant information)—what if your topic merits other types of research methodologies?

Interviewing and Field Research: Generating Your Primary Data

You may find yourself involved in a research project—perhaps, say, in anthropology or oral history, to name just two—that will require you to interview or observe others. Volumes have been written on the art of the interview, for instance, and clearly, there will be examples of best practices online. You might also need to conduct a survey; you may find you need to generate field notes. But how do you know you are approaching these other types of information gathering in the best way possible? What follows is a very brief overview of some fairly complex forms of information gathering.

Here are some tips for generating the raw data that you will incorporate with other sources. For field notes, jottings or observations that are collected at a specific site that is relevant to your research topic:

- Try to refrain from participating in the activities you are there to record; this will allow you to take the role of the observer and researcher.

- Write as much as you can while you are at the site, and save for later your "weeding" of what was important and what wasn't.
- Consider all of your senses: what you hear, smell, see.
- Remember that it can be as important to record your reactions to what you see as it is to record what you see. Be mindful of your own responses, but remember to keep observing and recording.

For interviews, the art of engaging with someone else or others to record their thoughts and observations on a particular subject with which they likely are familiar:

- Enter the interview informed. Know something about the person you're talking with and be sure you have context regarding the subject about which you're interviewing them.
- Have a script of informed questions that allow you to stay focused and on point.
- When appropriate, go off script to help your subject be comfortable; ask follow-up questions that might lead to something revelatory or new about your subject.
- Avoid double-barreled or leading questions that seem to entrap or force a certain kind of response from your interviewee. Open-ended questions will actually allow you to the kind of response you need.
- Be skeptical of your technology. Assume that your recording device will fail and have a backup—even if that backup also includes a pad and pencil.

Remember that if you do a very good and through job, your interview material may well become fodder for additional presentations or research opportunities.

For survey research, the opportunity to ask short, simple questions of potentially large audiences:

- Know your audience and choose the form of dissemination best likely to reach them.
- Develop questions that require short answers and that will encourage your audience to take the time to respond.
- Consider using free, online survey tools (such as Survey Monkey) as a way to reach particular audiences, keeping in mind that for some types of audiences, you may need to send hard copy to ensure access.
- Allow yourself enough time to collect multiple responses with survey research; you want to make sure you have plenty of lead time before your deadline.

These forms of data gathering will complement other materials and resources that you find—even more traditional sources such as books. The following activity will assist as you determine what types of sources and data you might need.

Ideas Into Practice

What kinds of sources do you need? It depends on the discipline and your subject, but here are some possibilities.

Different disciplines expect different kinds of sources and even expect certain types of conventions in writing that may differ from others' expectations. For instance, scholars in literary studies more often than not use the present tense when discussing an author's work, as the *work itself still exists* (as in "Charles Dickens says . . . "). Historians, on the other hand, more often than not will use the past tense (as in "Presidential historian Max Beschloss said . . ."). We will remind you of these examples again later on.

As researchers make sense of the sources they have, categorize yours according to the conventions of your subject as primary or secondary sources. This is just a partial list, and you might consider creating the equivalent of a spreadsheet to record and question the relevance of the various sources you have thus far:

Anthropology: Recordings, films, scholarly articles and books (secondary), first-person narratives and documents; qualitative data.
My source:
Relevance:

Literary Studies: The primary subject itself (the novel, poem, story, etc.); scholarly articles (secondary); author manuscripts and letters; and possibly, reviews written at the time the work was published.
My source:
Relevance:

History: Scholarly books and articles; narratives, documentation of witness accounts.
My source:
Relevance:

The Sciences: Laboratory reports; data in a variety of quantitative forms (graphs, tables, etc.); data from one's own laboratory work and/or survey results.
My source:
Relevance:

CHAPTER seven

Yours, Mine, or Ours? Integrating Resources

talking points

- I've done all of my research. Now what?
- How can I use both my own ideas and those from my resources?
- How do I summarize?
- How do I paraphrase (without plagiarizing)?
- When should I use a direct quotation?
- What is "patchwriting" and how can I avoid it?

You have chosen a research topic, you have spent a lot of time conducting research and collecting resources, and now it is time to answer the next big question: How do you use all of the information you have? That is, how do you integrate the resources you have found into your own research writing?

From Research to Writing

In this chapter, we will help you explore the various ways in which you can incorporate research material into your own work—your paper. Namely, we will discuss the ins and outs of summarizing, paraphrasing, and direct quotation—the primary skills you will need when engaging resources.

Beginning the Conversation

As we have mentioned, writing a research essay is not unlike having a conversation with others—in this case, your academic peers. Many ideas—many voices—come together in your work. Therefore, as with any conversation, one of your primary tasks must be to recognize when you should enter the conversation and when you should let others do the talking.

Ultimately, as the research writer, it is your job to shape the conversation; you develop the framework within which everyone else's ideas (your resources) are contained. We often tell our students that this kind of balancing act can sometimes lead to a bit of tug-of-war within the writing. It is very easy for research writers, especially beginning research writers, to lose control of their essays; they let the resources take over.

As you read this chapter, however, it is very important to remember that your research writing must depend on your own words and ideas. You are not simply a patchwriter, quilting together the ideas of others (something we will talk more about a little later). You are responsible for conceiving of and constructing your own argument, and you will need to make use of the resources you've collected to help *support*—not *create*—that argument.

Let's talk about how to begin.

89

Integrating Resources: Summarizing, Paraphrasing, and Quoting

Summarizing

You are likely already familiar with how to summarize. This is one of the first skills we learn as we are taught to engage with texts and to recount our understanding of what we've read. That is, at some point when you were in school, you were undoubtedly asked to read a book. And, to hold you accountable for having done that reading, a teacher probably asked you to tell the class what the book was about. You were asked for a summary.

We summarize the resources we use to construct our own research arguments for much the same reason. Just as your teacher needed to make sure that you read and understood your assignment for class, your essay's audience needs to make sure that you read and understood the resources you have chosen to include in your paper—and that you have employed them appropriately.

A good summary—the kind of summary necessary for academic writing—shows that the researcher has a firm grasp on and is able to readily identify what is important in a resource. It shows that you, as an accountable, smart writer, can read, understand, and then synthesize resource material to the benefit of your own essay and the argument you want to advance.

Paraphrasing

To paraphrase is to communicate the ideas in a resource, using your own language. Much like summarizing, paraphrasing, when done well, shows the audience that you are able to clearly and accurately explain what you have read in a resource without relying too excessively on direct quotation.

Further, paraphrasing can help the researcher to contextualize and support an argument. It allows the writer to offer overviews of the source material without surrendering control of the essay to another scholarly voice (or a set of scholarly voices). In addition, paraphrasing can keep your paper from appearing to be merely a set of connected quotations with no contribution of your own ideas—and without these attributed, summarized ideas.

However, it is in their attempts to paraphrase that we see many of our students verge dangerously close to plagiarism. Often student writers struggle with making their own paraphrased sentences differ enough from the original text in a satisfactory way.

When a reader can spot overlaps in language and/or sentence structure between your essay and the original source, it can hurt your credibility (and your ethos) as the researcher. These sorts of similarities, which students often claim are unintentional and which sometimes actually are unintentional, can be mistaken for plagiarism.

For example, let's look at the following passage, which reproduces our earlier paragraph:

> When a reader can spot overlaps in language and/or sentence structure between your essay and the original source, it can hurt your credibility as the researcher. These sorts of similarities, which students often claim are unintentional and which sometimes actually are unintentional, can be mistaken for plagiarism.

The following attempt at paraphrasing actually plagiarizes the original text:

> Readers can spot overlaps in language and/or sentence structure when they look at your essay and the original, and it can hurt your credibility. Even if you claim that this is unintentional, it can be mistaken for plagiarism.

This next paraphrase verges on plagiarism:

Students often unintentionally plagiarize when attempting to paraphrase a resource. Readers can easily spot this kind of plagiarism by finding overlaps between your essay the original source.
(Holdstein and Aquiline 101)

Although this writer has cited the source, the attempt to paraphrase isn't careful enough, and the writer would do well to use a direct quotation.

And this final attempt, which does not plagiarize, successfully paraphrases the original text:

As Holdstein and Aquiline warn, one of the ways students can ensure that they are not plagiarizing the original source is to paraphrase very carefully. Students should move beyond simply rearranging words or changing sentence structure and make sincere attempts to communicate the ideas of the original source without relying on the same language—unless they are using direct quotes. If your language looks too much like the language of the original, the reader can often tell, and students may be accused of plagiarism.
(Holdstein and Aquiline 101)

Direct Quotation (Quoting)

When you use the exact language of a source, and you include that language in your essay verbatim, you are quoting. Direct quotes are usually easy to spot in an essay, as they are surrounded by quotation marks as an indication that the words and ideas are taken from a research source and did not come from the research writer him or herself.

When students first begin writing the results of their research, they tend to rely very heavily on direct quotation. This seems to be the case, primarily, because student writers have difficulty establishing and owning their own voices—something we discuss at the beginning of this book. (However, we know that it is sometimes also an attempt to increase page length.)

Therefore, we encourage our students to use direct quotes sparingly, suggesting that they only quote a source directly if the original phrasing is integral to the overall idea or points they are trying to make. Similarly, only use a direct quote when the language in the source is as important as the idea being communicated.

Avoid Patchwriting

Being highly selective of how and when you choose to incorporate direct quotations will help you avoid *patchwriting*. Patchwriting—sometimes referred to as quilting—occurs when the writer relies too heavily on resources, excluding his or her own ideas and analysis. What results is something akin to a quilt of quotes devoid of any sort of thesis, analysis, or synthesis from the writer. Again, it is important to remember that you are using quotations from sources to support *your* argument; your essay cannot be composed of only source material.

Use the Quote Sandwich

One of the best ways to avoid patchwriting—and one of the best methods for using quotes in your essay—is to learn to make a *quote sandwich*. Rather than including a quotation in your essay with little or no analysis or explanation, make sure to sandwich each quote with your own words and ideas. Your top "piece of bread" should include a few lines introducing the relevance of the quote and providing any contextualization. Your bottom "piece of bread" should include a few sentences explaining and analyzing the quotation. For example:

> In their book, *Who Says: A Writer's Research*, Holdstein and Aquiline emphasize the importance of avoiding patchwriting, suggesting

that research writers should "make sure to sandwich each quote with [his or her] own words or ideas" (Holdstein and Aquiline 85). Using a quote sandwich can help researchers maintain control of their writing, assuring that they use text from resources as a way to support and not replace an argument.

In this example, you can see that the direct quote is *sandwiched* between sentences that introduce and explain the quote. In addition to the quote sandwich, you might also find it helpful to remember the acronym ICE: introduce the quote (using the signal phrases we discuss next), cite the quote, and then explain the quote in your own words. Remembering to use quote sandwiches—or the ICE method—will ensure that you are properly contextualizing the words from your sources within your own argument, using your own language.

Using Signal Phrases

A *signal phrase* is a word or group of words that introduce a piece of information from a text or a direct quotation.

It is important that you use signal phrases regularly, as they will let your audience know when you are integrating material from one of your resources and when you are engaging with the ideas of other scholars. Using these phrases regularly will help keep you accountable and honest.

We encourage you to not only use signal phrases but also to experiment with the language you use is these phrases. Resist the urge to rely on the same old signal words again and again (e.g., "Jane Smith says").

While there are many to choose from, and we encourage you to create your own list of verbs to use in signal phrases, here are a few to help you get started: admits, agrees, argues, asks, believes, calls, claims, comments, confirms, defines, denies, declares, echoes, emphasizes, estimates, finds, illustrates, implies, mentions, notes, predicts, proposes, reasons, recognizes, refutes, responds, reveals, states, suggests, tells, thinks, warns, writes.

Summarizing, Paraphrasing, and Direct Quotation: Knowing Which to Use and When

When is it appropriate to summarize, paraphrase, and quote directly?

It's best to paraphrase and summarize when the wording in the original source seems less important than the ideas or meaning of that source. Using both of these techniques will allow you to maintain your own voice in the paper and a kind of rhetorical consistency—that is, the approach to the argument as determined by the way you have established the sound and feel of the paper rather than the voice of the experts you're quoting.

Another benefit of summarizing and paraphrasing is that they will allow you to provide an overview of extensive and complex sources that may be essential to your argument but whose details are less important for the reader to know.

On the other hand, as we have mentioned, choose to quote directly when the wording of the original source is as important as the meaning. When the original text communicates a complex or significant idea—or if the passage is a particularly famous one, if not common knowledge—and if accuracy is especially important, then be sure to quote the passage directly. Quotes of one to three sentences in length should remain in the body of the paper, while longer quotes should be made into "block quotes" set apart from the body of the paper. Block quotes are often formatted differently, depending on your citation style. So be sure to check for the particular conventions of the style within which you are working.

Table 7.1 charts the ideas articulated in this chapter in a succinct chart that you will find useful as a checklist.

Think of integrating sources as entering into a complex set of conversations—or better yet, think of yourself as the symphony conductor who is also playing the piano. Find a way to enter this conversation by acknowledging others' contributions that have brought you to your own argument; as the pianist-conductor, you're integrating and acknowledging others' contributions to the whole while engaging in your own contributions to the conversation as well.

Table 7.1

METHOD	HOW DO I DO IT?
Summarizing	• Briefly explain the main ideas, key concepts, and arguments found in a source. • Strive for concision. Only include what is necessary for your own essay and your argument. • Read the source thoroughly to assure that your summary is both accurate and ethical. • Include a citation that identifies the source of the information you have summarized. • Make sure to clearly differentiate between your own ideas and the ideas from your resource.
Paraphrasing	• Reword or rephrase the information in a source, communicating the source's ideas using your own language. • Make sure to complete the translation, avoiding any overlaps in wording or sentence structure with the original source. • Read the source thoroughly to assure that your paraphrase is both accurate and ethical. • Include a citation that identifies the source of the information you have paraphrased. • Make sure to clearly differentiate between your own ideas and the ideas from your resource
Quoting	• Use the exact words from a source, making sure to use quotation marks appropriately. • Be very selective about how and when you choose to directly quote a resource, only doing so when the exact language from the source is integral to the meaning. • Make sure to sandwich each quotation with your own explanation and analysis. • Avoid taking a quote out of context. Make sure that you accurately represent the original author's intent. • Include a citation that identifies the source of the quotation.

Ideas Into Practice

Select a key resource that you've identified in your working bibliography. Length of the source doesn't matter; for this activity, if you select a longer book, for instance, you will have determined which section of a longer piece is useful to you.

After carefully reading and annotating this source, communicate the main ideas of the passage in three separate ways, using the methods we've suggested in these pages:

Paraphrase the portion of text you have selected; then
Summarize the portion of text you have selected; then
Directly quote aspects of text you have selected.

This activity might seem a bit redundant; however, it will illustrate how you should use these various techniques appropriately when integrating ideas and source materials. By comparing the three, you will have a sense of how each is most effectively used and when it might be appropriate to use one instead of another.

CHAPTER eight

Now I Have Evidence: Writing and Crafting Your Research

talking points

- What should I do with all of my notes?
- Do I need to write an outline for my research paper?
- What should be included in that outline?
- How do I know when I am ready to begin writing?
- How should I structure my essay?

One big advantage of good note taking—something we have stressed several times throughout this book—is that you will be able to organize and outline your research paper much more efficiently with thorough notes in hand than if you have few or no carefully written notes at all. Instead of starting from scratch to figure out what in the world you will write, your note cards and various jottings should serve as the scaffolding on which you construct the first draft of your essay.

Organizing and Strategizing

Therefore, before you begin writing, you should first organize all of the materials you will use to craft your outline—the road map for you as a writer, the results of which will guide your reader through your argument. Don't be afraid to take over the kitchen table or your dorm room floor. While surrounding yourself with your many resources and notes may irritate your roommate, having a chance to survey everything visually—to take it all in, if you will—will help you begin working on a draft.

Part of the organization process also involves differentiating between ideas that you will glean from your many resources and ideas that you have been able to craft and to synthesize from your many hours poring over resources in the library, on the Internet . . . or wherever you have found (and made note of) them. Again, surveying all of the resources you have accumulated, organizing them prior to drafting, will keep you credible and accountable—and on track. And consider that this type of review of your notes and resources may also help you determine whether there are any gaps that might send you back to the library or to the Internet.

From Notes to an Outline

Just as we urged you to do some pre-searching before you began crafting your research question, we also urge you to do some prewriting before you begin the drafting process. Outlining, for instance, is a form of prewriting. As with any kind of essay writing, it is extremely helpful to do some kind of outlining to help you envision the paper, and this outline can take the form of a list, if you so choose.

The expectations for writing about a research question are no different than the expectations for any other essay—only higher. The audience will anticipate that you will clearly articulate your argument, support your argument through both your resources and your own ideas, and make use of those resources both ethically and credibly.

So it is all the more important that you make sure to carefully and thoughtfully plan your research paper.

An outline will help you structure that work, and it will provide that all-important road map for you as you move forward with the writing process. That said, however, remember that some writers prefer to start drafting after they've organized their materials, turning to an outline or list (or précis, which we will discuss) when they find themselves stuck or in need of more planning. Writing is more often than not a nonlinear process.

Your outline may vary according to the nature of your particular assignment, but it should do the following:

> *Return to both your initial research question and thesis statement.*
> A good thesis statement, as we have discussed earlier in the book, should precisely and concretely articulate the argument that you

intend to support in the essay. Including the thesis in your outline will help you return to the framework you initially established for your research. Why were you originally interested in this topic? What did you want to explore? What questions did you want to answer? The answers to these questions—many of which you asked at the start of this project—should help guide you as you organize your paper.

Express both your argument and your supporting claims.
As you move into the writing stage of the research process, you will need to be able not only to give your argument but also to support your argument. Your outline should include all supporting claims and evidence in the order you wish for them to appear in the essay. In other words, make your argument, explain the reasons for your argument, and then provide your audience with evidence, which will mostly come from your resources. Typically, arguments tend to be ordered in sequence from weakest to strongest, so that your research paper ends in the strongest possible way before you tie together your work in the conclusion.

Include the ideas you want to integrate from each resource.
Your outline is the place where, if you have taken good notes throughout the research process, your hard work should begin to pay off. These notes will not only indicate which sources you will be citing from, but—if you followed our note card model in Chapter 3—these notes should also indicate exactly which of the concepts, ideas, and direct quotes from the source you will include in your paper.

Since the most useful outlines are usually concise, you won't need to include the full quotation or summary from the text. Instead, you will want to write something like "include quote from Smith, page 53," or "stuff from note card number 12," or "discuss Rich's theory of feminist poetics." The point is, of course, that your outline should indicate what you want to say and where you want to say it—and how.

Explain what you learned.
If you were conducting scientific research, you would want to make sure that the end of your outline makes note of the results of your study. However, since you're probably grappling with the kind of conceptual research topics we discussed in prior chapters, you likely won't be revealing or analyzing any quantitative data. Nonetheless, it is important that you begin to flesh out your concluding ideas. What did you find throughout the research process? What conclusions did you come to? What was revealed to you (and, in turn, to your audience)?

Keep in mind, moreover, that there is no one, single, desirable structure for an outline, unless your instructor requires a particular format. In what one of us calls "the old days," instructors would often demand a rigorous template: Begin with roman numeral "I," use subhead "A," followed by sub-subhead "1," and then lower case "a," and so forth. You needn't—unless your instructor expects it, again—structure your outline in this way. Some writers use a topic-based outline; others use bullet points or sentences that remind them of the direction they wish to take.

The Anti-Outline

All that said, some of us find outlines not only difficult to do— acknowledging that writing is often a recursive process of discovery, that it is not linear—but counterproductive. In that case, consider writing a *précis* (pronounced prey-see) that encourages you to summarize what you believe your research paper will be about after you've reviewed and thought about all of your materials. Then, you can work backwards, so to speak, from there: "If my summary says X and Y, then I will use A and B to begin to argue that point of view." You will need to be very familiar with your research materials and have some sense of the direction of your paper (something we recommend anyway) to do this.

Even if you are not writing a précis of your own essay, you can create a précis for most of the key entries in your bibliography, summarizing each of those articles or books or other sources concisely, clearly, and coherently. These summaries will help you think critically about how to best use these sources and incorporate them in your paper, and they will be useful if your instructor requests an annotated bibliography, a bibliography that features a short paragraph or so about each entry, delineating the main point(s) of the source and indicating its relevance to the overall topic and focus of the paper.

The bottom line: Sketch things out on paper (hand-written or digital) as a type of list or group of summaries that will help you draft your essay. Make sure it's a list that you can access with ease anytime you want to consult it—in a hard-copy notebook or on a jump drive or a tablet that you always have with you.

Begin with Your Bibliography—Standard or Annotated

The Standard Bibliography

Because students usually dread writing their bibliographies, they often save this task until the very end of the writing process, often throwing them together right before they submit the final essay to the instructor. (There is more information about bibliographies and citations in the next chapter.)

In truth, it is best to begin your bibliography during the initial stages of the research process. As we'll discuss in the chapter that follows, there are many online resources—which are both user friendly and free to the public—that you can use to track your sources as you collect them and that will also assist your putting these sources in the appropriate format. Since these online bibliographies are easy to amend, you can (and should) add and subtract from them as you refine your final lineup for your bibliography.

Starting the writing process with a working bibliography will not only help you keep mental track of the many texts from which you are summarizing, paraphrasing, and quoting, but having the bibliography will also help you write your in-text citations (something else that we'll discuss in Chapter 8).

So start your bibliography, print it out, and have it near you as you draft.

The Annotated Bibliography

As you write, you will want to ensure that you are able to articulate fully and carefully the ideas expressed in the resources you have chosen to include in your bibliography. In other words, before you begin incorporating a source in your essay draft, you want to first make sure that you can summarize its key points.

As we mentioned earlier, an annotated bibliography allows you to do just that. Annotated bibliographies include not only the requisite information necessary for a citation (author, publisher, dated published), but they also include a brief summary outlining main ideas.

Here's an example of an annotated citation:

Pollan, Michael. *The Omnivore's Dilemma: A Natural History of Four Meals*. New York: Penguin, 2006. Print.

Pollan's book explores the paradox that is the American diet. He examines not only what we eat, but he also attempts to explain how we have devolved into a country that supports an unhealthy and unethical food system—one that isn't environmentally sustainable. Pollan approaches this book through an interdisciplinary lens, relying on history, science, and personal experience to make his argument.

105

Instructors will often ask for an annotated bibliography as part of the process toward your final research paper as a way to have you (and for the instructor) to examine the appropriateness and depth of your research. Sometimes this annotated bibliography is included with the final paper; this is up to your instructor.

Coming Up with a Title

Much like the bibliography, many students wait until the end of the writing process to come up with a title. While you don't want to title your paper too soon—sometimes we don't know how things will turn out until we finish drafting—coming up with a working title at this point can help you focus your paper. Conversely, it can also help you test the evidence you'll use to defend your argument—and it may mean that you need to retool the title.

Further, writers may find that a clear title will help get them started; having articulated a focus (even if it needs redoing later on) might help conquer the blank screen or page. While there is no absolutely correct way to create a title, it has become customary in many disciplines to have a two-parter. That is, the first part preceding a colon is the attention-grabber, or the larger part of your argument, while the part after the colon is more specific. Here are some examples:

Caffeine-Crazed: Race and Coffee Culture(s) in the United States
Taming the Tyranny of Fashion: The Iconography of the High-Heeled Shoe

Of course, the colon is not mandatory, and to many, the two-part title has become something of a cliché. You can always craft suitable title without the two-part format:

Masculinity and the Cultures of Video Games in the 1980s
The Decline of Female Professors in STEM Disciplines

Once you have a working title (remember, you can always change it, and it's likely that you will), you can begin the process of drafting your paper.

Planning and Drafting

Are you ready to begin writing? Perhaps. Perhaps the outline or précis (or sketch, or however you are conceptualizing your work) isn't even finished, but you find yourself just itching to start drafting the first part of your paper, and you want to see where your writing takes you. That's fine; for many, writing, as we've noted, is a very recursive and often nonlinear process.

RESEARCH

WRITING

But do as much of that outline as you can—just in case it helps you later on. And, indeed, if you're eager to give the writing a try, it could be just because you want to test the proverbial waters and see if you are, indeed, prepared to begin drafting the entire paper. (We will acknowledge that some of us actually begin to write "in our heads" once we have gathered and reviewed the research materials and generated the focus of the paper—and the main argument. This makes us ready to begin the drafting process, but of course, this isn't the case for everyone.)

You will know you might be ready to begin drafting your research essay when:

- You have spent a considerable amount of time gathering, surveying, and analyzing various resources.
- You have a developed and focused thesis statement or research question.
- You have considered what your thesis statement promises and whether you are able to "make good" on that promise.
- You have considered both your ethos as a research writer and the audience you are either explicitly or implicitly addressing through your work.
- You can identify not only your supporting arguments but also the evidence with which you will back your claims.
- You understand what you have learned as a researcher and what your audience will learn from reading your essay.
- You have written an outline (you may also call it a "list") that orders the various topics and sources that you will use to prove your argument.
- You understand and accept that you may not have the perfect introduction to your argument just yet: Sometimes you have to finish the paper to know what it is you'll be introducing, so don't let the introduction stop you. You can add that later.
- You find yourself eager to test all of the work you've done with a "dry run"; or, conversely, you aren't that eager. Either way, it

might be time to see whether your materials are ready, your thesis is sound, and that your arguments and your evidence are well organized. It might just be time to plunge in.

Just as starting this project may have seemed overwhelming, so, too, will the blank page or screen seem overwhelming as you prepare to write. The hardest part, sometimes, is getting started. Be aware that even as you write, you will find yourself coming back, revising, changing, moving the order of things. This is all part of most writers' processes. Save punctuation, style, and other, similar concerns for later; gather your materials, and begin.

Ideas Into Practice

Now that you're aware of the annotated bibliography, take five or ten of your own sources and annotate them (remember your numbered note cards, whether paper or online) to illustrate to your instructor and to yourself what is important about them. Make sure to organize them in alphabetical order by the author's last name (just as you would in a standard bibliography).

Then, create an anti-outline, where you slate in order the annotated sources; this is also a good time to begin to figure out in what order these sources will appear in your work. Write several lines thinking through your decision-making process:

> For example, I'm going to begin with notecard 3 that has the quote from Mark Twain about honesty. This will help draw in my reader as I begin to write about ethics.

Or:

> On page two, as I began my own discussion of trade agreements, I will paraphrase Bill Clinton's quote about the NAFTA trade

agreement from note card 12. This will lead well into the political controversies surrounding his signing of the agreement.

In other words, you're doing the writing equivalent of "talking through" why you are making the choices you are making—a productive way to check yourself and your analysis of your resources. At the same time, you're actually developing a rough, outlined draft, if an incomplete one, that may prove useful to you later.

CHAPTER nine

What's Appropriate? Citing Sources and Citation Formats

talking points

- What are the various citation styles?
- Which style will I likely be using in my college writing class?
- What is a bibliography and how do I write one?
- In-text citations? What are those?
- What—exactly—needs to be cited?
- How do I cite a film? A book? An interview?
- Is it okay to use online citation guides?

In this chapter, we will provide you with a brief overview of academic documentation, focusing primarily on MLA and APA styles, respectively. The MLA style, recommended by the Modern Language Association of America, is most frequently used in disciplines within the humanities. It is the style that we personally have had the most experience with—both as teachers and as academics. It is also the style that you will likely be asked to use in many of your college writing courses. However, many of you will have encountered the style format represented by the American Psychological Association (APA)—and possibly others as well.

Understanding Citations

It is important, therefore, to acknowledge that there are myriad citation styles that are commonly used in academic writing, depending on the discipline. And the goal of this particular chapter isn't necessarily to make you an expert in either MLA or APA or Turabian style. Our goal, instead, is to help you understand *why* documentation is so important. To that end, we offer you an overview of some of these style formats rather than going into extensive detail about any one format in particular (see Table 9.1).

We also want to acknowledge that there are myriad resources online that will help you make certain that your bibliographic sources, your footnotes (if you have them), and your in-text citations are correctly formatted. As we hope and trust that you have reserved your intellectual energies for your thesis and your argument, we nonetheless want to help you be certain that you follow through on this important form of correctness and accountability.

Table 9.1   COMMON CITATION STYLES

STYLE	DISCIPLINES
MLA (Modern Language Association)	Literature, arts, humanities
APA (American Psychological Association)	Psychology, education, social sciences
AMA (American Medical Association)	Medicine, health, biological sciences
Turabian / University of Chicago	Various disciplines

Bibliographies (and Works Cited)

There is one surefire way that you can easily identify a piece of research writing: there will always be a bibliography or works cited accompanying it. Since research writing always relies on something outside of the author's own ideas, you can look to the bibliography to see exactly what that something (or set of somethings) is. That is, the bibliography—or works cited, depending on the terminology your instructor uses—lists the resources that a writer has used to craft his or her own research essay.

Although many will use these terms interchangeably, a bibliography is more often than not a comprehensive list of every source you consulted, while a list of works cited refers to those sources you actually used in the paper. Many instructors will ask that you provide both lists—and some will also ask for an annotated bibliography that will not only explicate each source in brief but that will also indicate the value of each source related to your topic.

As you have read elsewhere in this book, the bibliography isn't something that you really save until the very end of the project. You will have been looking at sources from the very beginning, and consequently, you will have been building your works cited list—although it appears at the end of the paper—from the very start.

When Should You Begin Creating Your Bibliography?

However you choose to organize your notes and information regarding your sources—your iPad, the notes feature on your iPhone or Droid, handwritten note cards, or the like—we have emphasized that it's essential to record and to record accurately the sources of your materials as soon as you find them. As we've indicated before, you can conceivably begin your actual bibliography, your official list of sources, as soon as you begin your research, saving both time and stress at the end.

Earlier, we mentioned online resources that aid in creating bibliographies. Sites such as *BibMe* and *KnightCite* help to create and save bibliographical citations. Using these various resources allows to you easily amend your bibliographical list whenever necessary. So, if you add a source to your bibliography and later decide that you won't be using it for your essay, you can always delete it. Remember that it's always easier to delete a source than it is to scramble to find the citation for a source you decide in the last minute that you need to include. (In fact, we even recommend keeping a "deleted source list" on your notepad or hard drive, just in case, or maintaining all of your sources on your note cards or their equivalent, even after you've assembled a working bibliography.)

The In-Text Citation

Having a working bibliography to use as a reference as you write your essay will also help you when it comes to in-text citations (the format for which we will be talking about next). Your bibliography not only organizes your sources in alphabetical order, but the individual bibliographic entries are also good indicators of what piece of information needs to come inside your parenthetical citations. Almost always, the piece of information that appears first in your bibliography—whether it is a title, a director's name, the editorial name, or the name of an author—is what belongs in your in-text citations.

For example, let's say the following is a source listed in your bibliography:

Gold, Janet. *Why Bibliographies Are Useful.* New York: Good Research Press, 2003.

In this case, the very first piece of information is the author's last name. Therefore, a parenthetical citation in MLA format would look something like this: (Gold 23).

Say, instead, your bibliographical listing looked like this:

"Being an Accountable Researcher." *English Student Magazine.* May
2012. 23– 28.

In this particular entry, you can see that there is no identifiable
author of the article. So, rather than the author's last name, the in-
text citation—again, in MLA format—would include the title of the
article: ("Being an Accountable Researcher" 25).

> *Quick Fact*
> *What we now call the MLA Handbook for Writers of Research
> Papers (Seventh Edition, no less, at 292 pages) was first conceived as
> the MLA Style Sheet, primarily as a way to prepare manuscripts for
> publications. The modern-era MLA Handbook evolved from its
> then-new incarnation in 1971.*

Formatting In-Text Citations

In-text citations are just as they sound: citations that are placed within
the body of your essay. They are visual and logical markers, indicating
to your reader when and where you are integrating intellectual material from one of your sources, whether directly quoted or not. In short,
they signify when you are using ideas or words that are not your own.

Therefore, in a research paper, it is common to have many in-text
citations, although one is warned (again) not merely to string quotations and citations together and avoiding the kind of "patchwriting"
we discussed earlier in this book. In fact, while we always tell our
students that it is best to err on the side of excess—in other words,
if in doubt, use a citation—we reiterate that there is also a need to
balance the number of quotations or citations in the essay with your
own, appropriately conceived words. Most instructors will forgive an
extra citation or two. However, if you forget to use a citation where
one is needed, that mishap could be mistaken for plagiarism.

In-text citations are usually formatted as either footnotes or
parentheticals. Both MLA and APA, the two styles that seems

to prevail in academe and for which we will provide examples, use parenthetical citations. Although this may sound intimidating, it is really quite simple: as we illustrated earlier, a parenthetical citation is a citation situated within a parenthesis. (And when you hear the word "footnote," keep in mind that one type of footnote is used in some formats, albeit rarely, instead of in-text, parenthetical citations; however, in most forms of scholarly writing, the footnote is used as a way to provide additional explanation or to amplify a point made within the body of the essay or article. In this book, we write only of internal, parenthetical citation forms.)

In MLA format, your parenthetical citation will usually include the author's last name and the page number on which you found the ideas you discuss in any particular part of your essay. APA format, however, includes the author's last name and the publication date of the source you have referenced.

Let's look at some of the various occasions for citing sources, using both MLA and APA formats.

A Single Author

Most of the time, you will be working with resources that have a single author. Single-author citations are the simplest to document. Depending on the style format, you will include either the last name and the page number, or the last name, the publication date, and a page number of the particular source:

MLA Example: (Johnson 213)
APA Example: (Johnson, 1992, p. 198)

Note: While APA format doesn't require a page number for all citations—only when directly quoting a source—we find it to be a good idea to include one anyway. Fortunately, APA allows this as an option, one we prefer.

Two or Three Authors

If a source has two or three authors, you will all names, listing them alphabetically:

> *MLA Example:* (Adams and Goldblatt 297)
> *APA Example:* (Adams & Goldblatt, 2007, p. 297)

> or

> *MLA Example:* (Adams, Cole, and Goldblatt 297)
> *APA Example:* (Adams, Cole, & Goldblatt, 2007, p. 297)

Four or More Authors

In MLA, if a source has four or more authors, you include the name that would come first alphabetically, followed by "et al." ("and others" in Latin). In APA, if a source has six or more authors, you include the name that would come first alphabetically, followed by "et al." (For articles with five or fewer authors, you list all the author names the first time the source is cited, then use "et al." for subsequent citations.)

> *MLA Example:* (Patel et al. 26)
> *APA Example:* (Patel et al., 2011, p. 26)

Unknown Author

If an author's name is not listed—and this means that one is not provided at all, not that you can't find it—then you would include the title of the source inside of the parenthetical citation. If the title is long, it is acceptable to just use the first few words of the title. Remember, you must format the title appropriately, using either italics or quotation marks.

> *MLA Example:* ("Global Warming and Factory Farming" 26)
> *APA Example:* ("Global Warming and Factory Farming," 2001, p. 26)

Some Additional Tips about Formatting In-Text Citations

- If there is no page number on this original source, which often happens with online sources and websites, then you are not expected to include a page number in the citation.

- It is acceptable to include a span of pages in the citation. For example, if you were discussing ideas from pages 120–123 of a book by Emily Wong, your citation may look like this: (Wong 120–123) or (Wong, 2002, pp. 120–123). If you are using a direct quote, however, you should include the specific page citing the location of that quote. And you generally wouldn't want to span more than five pages in one citation. Remember, you always want to make it easy for your readers to trace the information you've cited back to the original source.

- Parenthetical citations are always a part of the sentence and never a part of the quotation. In other words, the punctuation for your sentence should come *after* the citation. Example: There is a direct correlation between the number of fast food restaurants in a community and the obesity rate (Porter 32).

- However, if you are directly quoting a source, the quotation marks should close *before* the citation begins. Example: White argues that "making sure people have access to healthy food choices is a community's responsibility" (129).

- If you use a signal phrase to introduce a quotation, that is, stating the author's name in a sentence (as we did in the example above), then you are not required to restate the name in the parenthetical citation. Instead, just put the page number (for MLA) or the publication date and page number (for APA).

- If a direct quotation is longer than three or four lines, then the quote should be formatted in what is called a "block quote." That is, separate the quotation from the text as in the instance that follows when the writer is quoting from the Norton Critical Edition of the Emily Bronte novel *Wuthering Heights*:

> Heathcliff went up once, to show her Linton's will. He had bequeathed the whole of his, and what had been her, moveable property to his father. The poor creature was threatened, or coaxed, into that act during her week's absence, when his uncle died. The lands, being a minor, he could not meddle with. However, Mr. Heathcliff has claimed and kept them in his wife's right.... (223)

MLA style asks for double spacing throughout, as above; in APA style, the block quote is single spaced. You do not need quotation marks around block quotes; the fact of the block itself signifies its being a quotation. Remember: The name of the author would usually proceed the page number—223—unless the previous citation has identified the source as being the Bronte novel (Bronte 223).

In-Text Citations and the Academic Conversation

In-text citations serve a larger role within academic communities in addition to the function they serve in your paper. Not only do they hold you accountable as the research writer, but they also allow readers of your work to follow up on any particular resources that may interest them.

For instance, let's say that Professor X writes a research essay about climate change and the resulting effects on coastal communities in Alaska. Professor Y might read the essay, find a specific section that particularly interests her, and decide that she wants to know more. By looking at the in-text citation that Professor X originally included in his work, Professor Y is now able to identify the book, article, or multimedia resource from which this highly interesting idea originated.

This is a scholarly cycle we have mentioned many times throughout this book, and, by conducting and writing research, you are playing a key role in that cycle. Using citations appropriately and carefully will assure that your readers—and other scholars—are able to use your research as a springboard for their own.

What Needs to Be Cited?

You must cite *anything* and *everything* that has come from a resource. Any form of intellectual property must be honored by an in-text citation. So, regardless of whether you are directly quoting, paraphrasing, or summarizing, if the information did not come from you, you must cite it.

You will include a citation when you use:

- the original language from a source
- ideas from a source that you have put in your own words via paraphrasing or summary
- individual facts
- specific phrasing
- unique terminology
- any visual materials from a source (photographs, cartoons, charts, graphs, etc.)
- ideas from a speech, lecture, or interview
- ideas from a television show, movie, or documentary

Where Do the Citations Go?

As we have just discussed, you will need to cite any information that has come from a source regardless of whether you have quoted the source directly or put the ideas from the source into your own words.

Online Citation Guides

One of the reasons that we have chosen to provide such a brief overview of citation styles is that we acknowledge that so many citation resources are now readily available online. Citation guides—regardless of the style—are constantly updated and amended. So, in many ways, online resources—which can be updated easily and frequently—will often provide the most relevant and timely information when it comes to the various documentation formats.

Your instructor will likely point you in the direction of some reliable and credible online guides. (Remember our conversation about online resources from earlier in the book?) However, simply conducting a Google search for "MLA format" or "APA style" will yield multiple results, many of which will be of use to you.

Even more specifically, when you have questions about citation styles for a particular kind of source, Google may also come in handy. Searching for "how to cite a documentary in MLA format" or "how to cite an interview in Turabian" will often lead to the answers you are looking for.

In addition, many of the websites for your schools' libraries will include helpful information about citation styles.

So, as we have already mentioned, and as you likely know, the Internet can be an invaluable tool when it comes to academic documentation.

Ideas Into Practice

In the following list, we've deliberately left off any quotation marks or indications of formatting—and in some instances, we've left out the year the document or other item was published or produced. Use whatever citation format your instructor prefers and/or an appropriate online resource, and put the following in correct bibliographic format, researching any missing information as needed.

If you like, think of this as a bibliographic scavenger hunt of sorts:

Any essay in Best American Essays 1986
Abbey Road, the Beatles, 1969, Apple Corps
Alfred Hitchcock's Psycho
I Have a Dream (speech, not text)

Address Given on Inauguration Day, 1961

Season four, episode 12 of I Love Lucy

Interview with Barack and Michelle Obama by Barbara Walters

"The Feminist Fertility Myth," Slate, December 2012

Car Talk's final radio episode

Halo, Version 1, Xbox

Cover story, Ladies' Home Journal, March 1932

CHAPTER ten

What Now?
Revising, Presenting, Reviewing

talking points

- I'm done writing—now what?
- How can I revise my essay?
- What is peer review?
- What should I take into consideration when turning my essay in to my instructor?
- My instructor wants me craft a research essay presentation. What are my options?

Throughout this book, we have frequently discussed the various processes involved in writing about research: there is a process for choosing a topic, a process for gathering research, and a process for writing the research paper. As you approach the finish line, try not to lose sight of these processes, which, admittedly, don't necessarily follow in a straight line. That is, you might find yourself generating new content just as you've finished revising another section of your paper; you might find that you need to revise your introduction after you've made it to the conclusion; and so on.

And just because you have finished typing the conclusion, your research essay isn't necessarily complete.

The truth is, as much as we have encouraged you to engage with your instructors and your fellow researchers as you work through your projects, research writing can be—and often is—a solitary act. Ultimately, though, you have to make sure that your work is appropriate for a larger audience—whatever audience that may be.

So the final steps—the ones you will work through even after you may think you are "done"—are as important as any other. Before your research is prepared to make its debut, you must revise, review, and thoughtfully consider (and reconsider) the best methods for your written work along with the possibility of a presentation format of the same (or most of the same) information.

Revising

You might also want to approach your writing process, and consequently, your revising process, by thinking about both higher order concerns (HOCs) and lower order concerns (LOCs). HOCs are the more important and often more global areas of concern, such as idea development, clarity, focus, and purpose. LOCs, on the other hand, are instances that will likely be corrected during the editing of your essay (correcting word choices and commas, for instance), which will, in most cases, happen last. When editing for LOCs, you'll be looking to assure that you have a technically sound essay, free of mechanical and grammatical errors, and with appropriate word choices and structurally sound paragraphs.

Higher Order Concerns

You likely will want to begin by addressing HOCs. In a research essay, in particular, your HOCs will determine whether you have been successful in communicating and supporting your argument, organizing and developing your ideas, and integrating your source material into your essay.

Remember, writing a research paper is much like having a conversation, albeit a fairly formal one, both with scholars and with your audience. Now that your essay is drafted, you will want to begin asking yourself whether you are effectively participating in those conversations.

As you test your research and your writing, you may find that switching roles—imagining yourself as the audience for your essay and not the author of your essay—can be an effective way of determining whether you have written an essay that will meet the various needs of your readers.

Consider those HOCs, asking yourself the following questions:

- Have I clearly articulated my argument in thesis form? (Have I tried to distance myself from the thesis and asked, "So what?" Is my answer to that question satisfactory?)
- Am I able to adequately support my argument, using both my own ideas and ideas from my resources?
- Is my essay focused? Do I stay on task for the entire length of the paper, avoiding any digressions or tangents?
- Do I use transitions between ideas and between paragraphs?
- Are my paragraphs logical and structured well?
- Have I *developed* my paragraphs logically?
- Does each paragraph harken back to my overall thesis?
- Have I integrated my sources appropriately, avoiding quotes that are merely strung together?
- Is there enough "me" in the argument—that is, enough of my own commentary on the subject, balanced with appropriate attribution and quotation of sources?
- Have I avoided an abrupt ending to the paper, instead crafting a conclusion that summarizes my overall argument?

- Is my choice of language appropriate for my audience? How so?
- Have I made certain to avoid introducing new ideas or arguments at the point of the conclusion?

Lower Order Concerns

Once you are confident that your research essay satisfies all of the HOCs, you will want to focus on LOCs. This sort of editing will likely be the final step in the writing process, completed a day or two before the final essay is due. Although we're all familiar with the occasional need to wait until the last minute before assignments are due, it's undoubtedly best, especially when working on a comprehensive research paper, to leave yourself plenty of time—and especially at the end of the process. This way, you can wait a few days after you've completed the paper, giving yourself a bit of "distance," so that you're more likely to catch surface errors and other LOCs.

Additional Strategies

As with any kind of writing, you will want to read through your essay several times, employing whatever proofreading strategies have worked for you in the past. Here are a several editing strategies—strategies specifically designed to address LOCs—that we have used both with our students and with our own writing. While this list isn't meant to be exhaustive, we hope it will help you get started:

Read Your Essay Aloud

It seems to be the case that whenever we ask students to read their work aloud in class, they stumble over several of their own errors. When we read our own work out loud, we often are able to identify many of the typos, grammatical mistakes, and punctuation errors that we would otherwise overlook when quickly scanning our essay and "reading it" in our heads.

So, as silly as it may seem, read your essay out loud either to yourself or to a roommate. Doing so will often help you "hear" and find places where you will need to make adjustments or corrections—and your listener may be able to help.

Read Your Essay with a Particular Edit in Mind

Because LOCs are so wide ranging, it can be very difficult to try to catch and to edit all of the missteps in your essay with a single reading. After all, how can you expect to identify spelling errors, misplaced commas, and incorrect citations all at the same time? It's likely that you can't. (For that matter, neither can we.)

So, instead, read through your essay with a very specific editing goal. For example, if you know that you have a tendency to misuse commas, read through your essay and *only* pay attention to comma usage. Or, if you want to be certain that you have correctly cited all of your resources using MLA format, read through your essay and *only* look at your citations. While you may catch other errors and make them for a return visit, you won't initially be trying to do everything at once.

The point is this: the more you refine what specific changes or corrections you may need to make, the more likely you are to find those specific instances. Don't overwhelm yourself by trying to do it all at once.

Exchange Essays with a Classmate for Peer Review

No one knows the assignment for which you are writing better than your classmates. Like you, they have also spent the past several weeks sitting through class lectures, talking with your instructor, and working on their own research projects.

Therefore, when it comes time for you to revise and edit your complete draft, why not consult one of your peers? It is always a good idea to have another set of eyes read through your work before you turn it in, and you can return the favor by reading through your classmate's essay, too.

When revising either your essay or a classmate's essay during peer review, try to assess the work in stages, first paying attention to those HOCs and then, once you are confident that the essay is nearly complete, editing for LOCs.

So, as you approach your draft and work—or someone else's—to revise it, whether in class, online, or through other methods, consider these questions to test it: Have you presented your argument clearly and thoroughly? Is your choice of language suited to the argument and audience? Are your paragraphs well-organized, stemming logically from your thesis statement? Are your sentences grammatically correct, and have you edited for surface features (spelling and the like)?

Taking One Last Look at Your Thesis

Throughout the research process, and even as you write the first draft of your research essay, you will find yourself refining and revising your ideas. This is a necessary part of research writing, and this sort of revision is a habit of all good writers.

So, as you begin to finalize your essay, you will want to look back at your starting point: your thesis statement. Your thesis statement was initially crafted at the onset of your research. And, though you may have tinkered with it as you delved further into your various resources, you might still need to look at your thesis in light of your final essay.

When reviewing your thesis statement, consider the following:

- Does your thesis express a clear and declarative argument? How so?
- Do the resources you include in your essay provide evidence in support of your argument? How so?
- Have you narrowed and focused the thesis as much as possible? (Often the scope of your argument will narrow further and further throughout the research process.) Really?

- If someone else were to read your thesis statement and say, "So what?" and can still find an argument that's worth reading about, then you just might be on to something. If the "so what?" leads to indifference (unless you've happened upon someone who is just apathetic about everything), then you might want to take another, careful look.

Answering "yes" to these questions and being able to defend that "yes" likely indicates that you have a thesis that suits your final essay.

Presenting Your Research

As we mentioned earlier in this chapter, there comes a time in every research process when the work must be introduced to an audience. Sometimes that audience may only be your instructor. However, other times, you will be asked to present your research to a larger audience of your peers.

Research presentations can take many forms, and deciding what kind of presentation best suits both your project and your audience is, perhaps, the most important step. Therefore, when preparing a research presentation, ask yourself two questions: How can I best communicate the ideas in my work to a specific and targeted audience? And what presentation tools—multimedia or otherwise—are best suited to my topic, my audience, and the occasion for which I am presenting? As you approach these questions, it will be helpful to reflect back on our conversation about rhetorical situations earlier in this book.

As you begin to devise a game plan for your research presentation, here are some questions to consider.

What Is the Nature of the Presentation?

Are you presenting as part of a small conference, fair, or program that requires you to set up a visual display of you research? Or are you being asked to give a 5- to 10-minute summary presentation to your classmates? Clearly, your strategies will be different for each situation.

What Tools Are Best Suited to the Occasion for Which You Are Presenting?

If you are asked to set up a display at a small conference or research fair, you will likely make use of visual materials such as sophisticated poster boards, pamphlets, and brochures. However, if you are asked to do a timed presentation at the front of your class, you might want to consider using multimedia tools—like PowerPoint, Prezi, or iMovie—to help you communicate the most essential information from your research.

Which Multimedia Tools Are Most Appropriate for the Location in Which You Are Presenting?

You don't want to spend hours creating a striking video about your research topic if the classroom in which you will showcase your work does not have the technology to support your using that video as part of your presentation. When considering which multimedia tools you would like to use, make sure you speak with your instructor about the classroom's limitations and opportunities as a presentation space.

What Multimedia Tools Are You Comfortable Using?

This may seem counterintuitive, but your research presentation may not be the best opportunity to take creative risks.

That is, while it is important that you push yourself to make use of multimedia tools that can enhance your presentation and interest your audience, it is also important that you choose a tool that you can use effectively and efficiently. You don't want to find yourself getting so frustrated by a new presentation format that you lose sight of the quality of information you are presenting. This is all to say: keep your eye on the ball. The most important aspect of your presentation should be your research, not your video-making skills. So work to find a balance between using a new and innovative form of media and presenting your research accurately and thoroughly. Remember, the power may go out, but the fire of your research should not.

What Does Your Audience Already Know about Your Topic?

Most research presentations give a significantly abbreviated overview of the work. Therefore, you will want to present the major points of your research, focusing on the aspects of your topic that the audience won't already know. Ask yourself this: What does my audience already know about my topic? Are you speaking to a group of experts in the field related to your work? Or are you speaking to a more general audience? Is it necessary that you provide some background information? While you should provide the context necessary to foster your audience's understanding of your work, you should also be as concise as possible.

Keep your specific audience in mind when deciding what information you should or shouldn't include in your presentation.

How Can the Presentation Complement the Research?

Your presentation is an opportunity to bring in visual materials (images, video clips, excerpts from interviews, music, and the like) that are not readily conveyed in hard copy. Take advantage of the presentation to offer something that is not readily developed in the essay, moving beyond presenting excerpts of the text itself.

Therefore, while we have encouraged you to present the most salient points of the essay, take the opportunity to go a bit beyond for the purposes of a live presentation. For instance, digital versions of magazines such as *The New Yorker* make available related content such as interviews, videos, and photographs online that are not available with the print version of a story and that extend the story itself.

To reiterate: Consider both your topic and your audience as you select the most appropriate way to convey salient information about your work in a presentation format. No matter the format or software—a poster board, Prezzi, or movie-making software—the underlying principles of a good and sound presentation are the same. Know your audience, be prepared to convey the most important aspects of your research, and, if you use various media formats, be certain that they will be supported in your classroom and that they enhance but do not compete with the importance of your work.

132

The Final Checkup

Before you submit the final draft of your essay to your instructor, you will want to review your full project one last time, making sure that you have all the necessary components of the assignment and that you have presented the various components professionally. Ensuring that your project is presented appropriately—that all of your t's are crossed and your i's are dotted, if you will—contributes to your ethos as a responsible student and a trustworthy researcher. (Your instructor may begin to question your ethos, however, if you turn in your final paper with a coffee mug stain on the first page.)

As you do this final review, consider the following questions as you also review our advice throughout this book:

- Do you need a cover page? If so, what information should be included on the cover page?
- Is there a title that is both attention getting and informative?
- Are all parenthetical citations formatted appropriately?
- Are there any missing citations—information that should be accounted for but is not?
- Are your pages numbered?
- Have you included your bibliography? And is that bibliography formatted correctly?

Conclusion

Your instructor will undoubtedly have certain ways of assigning and supporting ways of conducting research appropriately and usefully, ways that pique your intellectual curiosity and as a budding researcher. In any event, the principles of careful, accountable research will carry beyond the classrooms through which you find yourself practicing its tenets, making you a more accountable, discerning citizen in the process.

Ideas Into Practice

Let's say you need to communicate aspects of your research paper to different types of audiences and through various media. In all these cases you must be fully aware of the unique rhetorical situation demanded by each.

How might you communicate the central ideas of your research paper as the following?

As a pamphlet for young adults?

As a conversation with a family member—with no background in the topic—across the kitchen table?

As a multimedia presentation—a Web page, a Prezi, or a PowerPoint—for your classmates?

As an instructional video of your research, including voice-overs, visual evidence, and presentation of quantitative data, for instance, for an educated, general audience?

As a summary memorandum to an executive who is interested in your ideas?

Afterword

What's Next? Tidbits for College and Beyond

We ask that you look forward to the research and writing that you will do in your other classes and in the workplace, but we also ask that you reflect on the foundational principles we have outlined throughout this book.

While there are certain conventions and nuances in every discipline that will differ from one to the other, remember that there are principles that transcend the field for which you are writing and researching: careful, through review of sources; accountable citation practices; your *ethos* as a writer, reflected in the care you bring to your writing and research; the importance of rhetorically strategic decisions as you consider audience, voice, diction, and the genre in which you are writing.

Therefore, as you come to this final chapter, think about the practices we've outlined not as skill specific to a first-year writing course but as wider ranging philosophies to carry forward in college and beyond.

Writing in Disciplines

After you have taken one or two semesters of first-year writing or another course of the sort that is often called "foundational," you will find yourself writing and researching in other content areas. You may, in fact, be writing in a variety of disciplines in your first college-level course.

Once you have to target your writing for other subject areas, you might be surprised: Why did your professor in, say, the English

Department tell you to use the present tense when referring to a text? We reiterate an earlier example to consider the following:

> "As Whitman *writes* in 'Song of Myself', he *is* 'large,' he 'contains multitudes.'"

However, your history professor will expect something else, based on the conventions of that discipline:

> "As historian Doris Kearns Goodwin *wrote* in *Team of Rivals*, Lincoln was a political craftsman who . . ."

These are examples of subtle, but significant disciplinary conventions that illustrate the potential differences among courses you will take or have taken, and these differences can also signal the wide-ranging types of writing you will find in your eventual workplace.

Professional Writing

You may not think of writing memoranda, e-mails, formal letters, re-sumes, reports, Web copy, and other, equally varied forms as you do the kinds of research writing you might do for your courses. However, much of what you will have done transcends the genre in which you're writing and is useful no matter the task or requirement.

While not all skills and strategies we've discussed will apply to every piece of writing you do in college or in your career, there are additional and basic principles that will apply: understanding your rhetorical situation; understanding and targeting your audience; as-suring the audience of your ethos as a writer; reviewing and evaluating your arguments for soundness and your prose for correctness; evaluat-ing carefully the sources that you use to help you make your arguments, if an argument is called for.

Further, be mindful of your process as you write. As you would for a research paper, consider, as noted earlier, writing a *précis* (pronounced "prey-see") that summarizes, for yourself, what the "story" of your research paper, memorandum, long e-mail, or other purpose for writing seems to be. Then, work backwards to create the document you need to create.

Therefore, while you're likely now writing for an audience of your peers and your instructor, there may come a time when you are writing for coworkers, your supervisor, your supervisor's supervisor, consumers, the diverse readers of your professional blog, or the like.

In sum, writing (and good writing) does not end with this particular writing project—or with this book. As we have noted earlier, the principles of good writing and research transcend any one assignment. We trust that the good work you will have done on your own, with your classmates, and with the guidance of your instructor will support and help you build toward other written and research-related work that you will do elsewhere in college and beyond.

Appendix

Sample Student Research Paper

We chose this student example to represent the result of a shorter research assignment. As we note several times throughout this book, there is no one correct way to approach research and writing, although this paper follows processes similar to those we describe and adheres to appropriate citation formats.

Of course, the nature of your assignment(s) may well be very different from this one, but perhaps this student's work will help you to react to decisions you assume the writer made about sources, the order of presentation, the central argument, support for the argument, word choices, and stylistic considerations.

As you read, consider the following questions and prepare to discuss your responses with your classmates after you complete your reading and analysis of the paper:

What is the writer's central argument—the writer's thesis? How is it conveyed? What might you have done differently—or not? How is the thesis supported? What are the supporting arguments?

In what ways is the writer able to establish ethos? Consider other forms of persuasion. Does the writer employ logos, for instance, to support arguments? How so?

Be mindful of the ways in which the writer integrates sources. Paying special attention to instances of summary, paraphrase, and direct quotation, how might you comment on the integration of source materials and the sources the writer chose?

Consider working backwards in analyzing this paper. That is, create a rough outline or anti-outline, as we've called it, attempting to discern the writer's process. What is the result? How does the paper seem to have been effectively constructed? How might it have been improved?

Comment on the writer's style and use of language. What, if anything, would you change?

Review the writer's citation formats and bibliography. Which citation format does the writer appear to use? How accurate are the citations and use of this particular format?

In fact, what is your overall assessment of the choices you can infer the writer made and their effects?

Nadezh Mayo

_____College

Gold-Diggers and Vamps:
Sexuality, Race, and Class in the Court Case
Rhinelander v. Rhinelander

On November 9, 1925, Leonard Kip Rhinelander, a wealthy member of the social elite from a well-regarded New York family, took his wife to court in an attempt to annul their marriage. Alice Rhinelander, born Alice Jones, fought the annulment, as newspapers and tabloids across America made a spectator sport of the emotional proceedings that unfolded over the next year. The seemingly happy couple, who had written many romantic letters during the three years of their courtship, hit a roadblock in their new marriage when a New York newspaper published a story claiming that Alice was the daughter of a "colored man." According to American ideas about race in the 1920s, that meant that Alice was black as well. Alice also worked as a nanny, and a scandal emerged when it became known that a famous Rhinelander had married a black servant girl. Although Leonard at first swore that he would stand by Alice no matter what the papers said and no matter her race, he soon changed his mind.

One year after their marriage, Leonard and Alice found themselves the central figures in the New York state court case *Rhinelander v. Rhinelander*. At the trial Leonard claimed that Alice had defrauded him by misrepresenting herself as white, and that he would never have married her if her had known that she had "colored blood" in her (Onwuachi-Willig 2401).

This particular case seems to have disappeared from popular accounts of history. It was not a Supreme Court case, and it is not as well-known as other cases pertaining to racial restrictions on marriage. (In fact, only two lawyers are known to have had access to the full court transcripts [2401]). For example, many people have heard of the case, *Loving v. Virginia*, in which an interracial couple from Virginia fought for the right to be together in 1967 and won, legalizing interracial marriage throughout the United States. The case of *Rhinelander v. Rhinelander* may not be as well known, but the trial is an equally important snapshot in American history. The court proceedings express American conceptions of race in the 1920s, as well as American ideas about the roles of men, women, and sexual boundaries in the context of race. To describe the trial as an attack on interracial marriage and the "pollution" of the white race by blacks is not wrong, but it is incomplete. Upon closer examination, the court case *Rhinelander v. Rhinelander*, although fought on the grounds of racial fraud, in fact has as much to do with sexuality and gender as it does with race. Indeed, it is nearly impossible to think about the *Rhinelander* case without addressing the important interactions of race, sexuality, and class in public perceptions of Alice—a poor, black woman.

The most immediate example of the role of sexuality in the *Rhinelander* case is Alice's reputation as a "vamp." Leonard's lawyer spent much of his energy trying to convince America that Alice was a sexual predator who had duped Leonard into marriage. The vamp was a popular female archetype of the 1920s. According to historians Earl Lewis and Heidi Ardizzone, ". . . the female vamp was overtly sexual

and always dangerous. . . . she did deprive them [men] of their power
and the predatory role of their social privilege. Men, not women, were
expected to be the sexual aggressors" (Lewis and Ardizzone 56). The
image of the vamp was not associated with women of color in particular, but there is certainly a connection between commonly held beliefs
about black, or partially black, women and the vamp. Women who
were of both white and black heritage, like Alice, were referred to a
"mulatto." Mulatto women were depicted as psychologically troubled.
"The female version of the tragic mulatto . . . accentuated her sexual
beauty" and had a "desire to gain power, wealth, or whiteness by sleep-
ing with white men" (29). The fact that mulatto women were seen as
sexual gold diggers with a manipulative streak explains why it was so
easy for Leonard's lawyer to convince the jury and the public to view
Alice as a vamp.

Alice's letters often contained references to sexual attraction or
sexual activity between herself and Leonard. She wrote one such letter
on November 17, 1921:

> Listen Lenard [sic], I have had some sweet hearts, but I have not
> loved them, like I have taken to you so. I have never let a fellow love
> an caress me, the way you do Lenard, because you make me feel so
> happy, and loyable [sic] toward you dear. But would it be awful if
> you had me my self alone. What you would not do to me. I can
> imagine. (Lewis and Ardizzone 89)

Another of Alice's letters, from May 19, 1922 reads, "I got undressed and got in bed which you can see me in bed like the Antoinette
[Marie Antoinette Hotel], and snuggled in bed. And read all of your
letters, but you made me feel very passionate for the want of you, telling me how happy my little hand as often made you feel, and several
other things, but can't help to tell you" (Onwuachi-Willig, 2436). By
expressing her sexuality, Alice showed herself to be a vamp in the eyes
of Mills and the public. The sexual content of her letters classified her

as sexually promiscuous, despite the fact that the letters were shared intimately between Leonard and Alice alone.

Leonard's letters were just as sexual as Alice's—more so, in fact, based on all the letters I have found. In July of 1922 he wrote, "Oh, Sweetheart, many, many nights, when I lay in bed and think about my darling girl, it [his penis] acts the very same way and longs for your warm body to crawl upon me, take it in your soft, smooth hands, and then work it up very slowly between your open legs" (Onwuachi-Willig 2433). One month earlier, in June of 1922, Leonard sent an even more explicit letter to Alice:

> Do you ever think, when you are lying in bed at night, how I used to make you passionate with my warm lips, and the way I did it? . . . Do you remember, honeybunch, how I used to put my head between your legs and how I used to caress you with my lips and tongue? . . . Oh! I often think when I used to lift up your night-gown and crawl down to the foot of the bed, so as I could be right under you. 'Please, dear, come.' Do you recall how I asked you to do that. (Smith-Pryor 153)

Compared to the detailed descriptions of Leonard's language, the suggested imaginings of Alice's letters are downright tame.

Yet only Alice was deemed sexually deviant for engaging in such talk. The discussion of Alice's status as a vamp in the courtroom and in the newspapers and tabloids shows how society attempted to police Alice's sexuality. The sexual content of Alice's letters served as more than a window into her sex life; it was meant to illuminate her character. Leonard's lawyer, Isaac Mills, painted Alice as a calculating, devious woman who preyed on Leonard's innocence (Lewis and Ardizzone 53). Because she had a sexual relationship with Leonard, the assumption was that she must also have been manipulative and a gold-digger, like the popular image of the mulatto woman. Alice's sexual activities dictated how every other aspect of her character was viewed. Many newspapers and tabloids echoed Mills's accusations about Alice's self-serving motivations behind her relationship with Leonard.

Perhaps surprisingly, Alice won the trial. The jury's decision to side with Alice and against Leonard is an expression of societal views on proper social conduct and racial roles. One way to read the outcome of the trial is that Leonard needed to be "punished" for his transgression of publically committing to Alice and cementing his relationship with her through marriage. And punished he was: After losing the trial, he was disinherited financially (although not emotionally) by his father, and died single at the age of thirty-four, "reportedly of a broken heart" (Onwuachi-Willig 2456). It may be said that in winning the jury's vote, Alice was rewarded for conforming the stereotype of a working-class black woman. For Leonard, a wealthy, white man, falling for Alice, who was poor and black, was scandalous in 1920s New York. Alice, though, did exactly what was expected of her. Society saw young black women as sexually indiscriminate and manipulative. Whether or not these words accurately describe Alice's actions, the allegation of being a vamp was brought against her in trial and in the media time and again. Like all poor black women of her time, the public already viewed her as a vamp even before her name appeared in the newspaper, by virtue of her race and class. While Leonard defied everyone's expectations of him as a wealthy, white gentlemen, Alice *confirmed* the expectations that the jury already had of her. Leonard betrayed his social position by marrying Alice, but Alice could hardly be faulted for acting according to her nature. In effect, Alice was rewarded for upholding the stereotype of black women as treacherous sexual vixens. Viewed through this lens, the trial's outcome—which at first glance may appear to have been a victory for the black community—was in fact both racist and sexist in its supporting conventional ideologies.

In light of Leonard's punishment for his relationship with Alice, it may appear that Leonard's sexuality was policed just in the way Alice's was. In reality, however, it was not Leonard's sexuality that was being policed, but something else entirely. Leonard was not attacked for his decision to have a sexual relationship with Alice; he was attacked for choosing to marry her even after learning that she was not entirely white. It was not acceptable for Alice to have a sexual relationship with Leonard before getting married. Once it was revealed in court that she had slept with him, every aspect of her character was called into question as a result. Her decision to have sex with Leonard introduced the possibility that she was a lying, selfish slut (to her detractors) who cared more about money than she cared about Leonard. At the same time, it *was* socially acceptable for Leonard to sleep with Alice outside the bounds of marriage. Premarital sex did not leave the same mark upon Leonard's character as it did on Alice's. Sex, for a man, is not viewed a *loss* of virginity the way it is for a woman, but a *gain* in masculinity and experience. Psychologists Michael J. Marks and R. Chris Fraley point out that the sexual double standard between men and women has long existed in Western societies, and that women are judged more harshly than men for having many partners (Marks and Fraley 20). Although Leonard's having sex with Alice without any specific plan to marry her was not exactly a source of conventional approval, it was not enough to destroy his character. As a man, and a white man at that, it was believed, if quietly so, that Leonard had an inherent right to sex that Alice was denied.

Leonard had a right to marriage as well as sex, but he threw that right away when he decided to waste (in conventional view) his social position on Alice. Leonard's choice in sexual practices did, in fact, come under attack: Lee Parsons Davis, Alice's lawyer, read a letter written by Leonard. This letter, referenced earlier in this paper, describes the act of performing oral sex on a woman, which Davis deems "an unnatural thing" (Smith-Pryor 154). However, although oral sex was frowned upon, Leonard's decision to engage in sexual activity of one form or another did not come under attack. It was entering the socially approved institution of marriage with Alice—not engaging in the taboo activity of premarital of sex—that sullied Leonard's good name. Indeed, many white men throughout history have engaged in sexual activity with black women. There are many examples of (often nonconsensual) sexual activity between male slave masters and their female slaves (Sonnen). As was the case for the men who came before him, it was acceptable for Leonard to have sex with Alice but it was not acceptable for him to validate their relationship through marriage. It was marrying Alice while presumably knowing about her racial background that posed a threat to Leonard's social status.

Sexuality factored into the *Rhinelander* case once again when Alice's lawyer, Davis, implied that a man could not be sexually assaulted by a woman. Davis joked dismissively that the accusations against Alice were "'. . . the first time I ever heard of a girl criminally assaulting a man'" (Lewis and Ardizzone 67). The question here is not the purpose behind his argument, but rather the idea that Davis put forth and the receptiveness of the jury to this idea. By siding with Alice, the jury showed that they most likely agreed with Davis's proposition that a woman cannot sexually assault a man. In Davis's eyes the thought of such a thing happening was not only laughable but also impossible. Regardless of whether Leonard and Alice Rhinelander's relationship involved any form of sexual assault perpetrated by either partner, the argument is a noteworthy one. This argument assumes that male and female sexuality, sexual practices, and potential sexual crimes are dictated by sex and gender alone; it presents the idea that a woman cannot be sexually aggressive and that a man cannot be a victim of sexual crime. Although it is possible for a woman to assault a man, and it does happen, this false belief still affects how we think about sexual assault today, and it helps to maintain the stigma against male victims of sexual assault (Pappas).

In what Lewis and Ardizzone refer to as "arguably the most memorable and troubling point in a trial already filled with drama and emotion" (Lewis and Ardizzone 156), Alice was asked to disrobe in court, baring her back, breasts, and legs for the jury and judge. Alice reportedly wept and had to be physically supported by her mother as she bared her naked body; later, she was so distraught that her father carried her out of the building. The purpose of the display, according to her lawyer, was to illustrate to the jury that Alice's body showed her obvious blackness and that therefore Leonard must have known that Alice was black before marrying her. Alice was humiliated in court—and in the countless retellings and visual reconstructions that followed—at the request of her own attorney, her advocate.

Relevant to this case is the charged racial and sexual past behind the public nudity of black women. The image of Alice's naked body

> . . . reverberates through a violent racial history and flickers with the remembrances of a multitude of atrocious vignettes: enslaved men and women standing on auction blocks, stripped before the examination of prospective purchasers; the icon of a half-dressed woman in chains on her knees pleading to her white abolitionist 'sister' for help; the 'Hottentot Venus,' a southern African woman named Sara Baartman, brought to England and put on display, usually nude, for scientific and curiosity-seeking audiences. . . . (Lewis and Ardizzone 156)

Alice was humiliated in a way that would never be inflicted upon a white woman; the fact that the court and public spectators already viewed Alice as black, and therefore inferior, allowed them to justify treating her in such a way. In the context of a long history of sexual degradation and public humiliation of black women, Alice's blackness in the eyes of her spectators made such a bodily display an acceptable course of action. Alice was part of a long line of African American women "asked or forced to bare her body to satisfy the needs and curiosities of white men" (Lewis and Ardizzone 157). Alice's treatment in this incident shows that the court already had a firm view of Alice as a sexual object.

Although the incident was private (no reporters were present), descriptions promptly appeared in the newspapers, including both fact-based retellings and vivid, dramatic imaginings. Many papers produced recreations of the scene in the form of sketches that depicted Alice partially naked. The *Evening Graphic*, however, outdid all other new sources when it published a photograph of the scene; the tabloid hired a model to pose as Alice, and then cut and pasted the image together with pictures from the actual trial. The composite photograph resulted in a highly sexualized—even pornographic—version of the event:

> The *Graphic*'s so-called composograph featured a half-nude Alice Rhinelander in front of her husband, the lawyers, the judge, and her mother with the caption, 'Alice disrobes in Court to Keep Her Husband.' Not surprisingly for the *Graphic* (referred to by its critics as the *Pornographic*), the paper sexualized the scene when it showed Alice in a scanty slip instead of the lowered coat described by the court stenographer. (Smith-Pryor, 204)

Alice's emotional and painful ordeal was distorted for the pleasure—sexual and otherwise—of the viewing public. Her story was told, retold, and extravagantly embellished for the fulfillment of onlookers, with little concern for Alice as a person. In the eyes of feminist writers Catharine MacKinnon and Andrea Dworkin, "objectification involves treating a person, someone with humanity, as an object of merely instrumental worth, and consequently reducing this person to the status of an object for use. The objectified individual is made into a tool for others' sexual purposes. Objectification, therefore, constitutes a serious harm to a person's humanity" (Papadaki). The tabloid obsession with discussing and recreating Alice's nudity devalued her humanity and focused all attention on her physical body alone; Alice was turned into an object to be played with, enjoyed, fantasized about, and tossed aside. It is important to note that, with the exception of her mother, Alice undressed in a room full of male spectators (for the judge, lawyers, jury, and stenographer were all men). This part of the trial reinforces then-socially acceptable expressions of male and female sexuality, in which men act and women are acted upon.

One way to view the disrobing debacle is as an indirect punishment for Alice. This is, of course, simply one view of many, but it is certainly worth considering how Alice's actions may have justified, in the eyes of her spectators, the unjust treatment that she suffered. The incident seems like an indirect punishment for metaphorically and physically baring all in front of Leonard and expressing her sexual urges to him in her letters. To reiterate, Alice was not passive in her relationship with Leonard. Just as Leonard was punished for committing to Alice—his racial and social inferior—Alice too was punished for failing to conform to societal expectations of her sexual conduct.

In one letter, Alice writes, "Len do you remember in old Marie Antoinette the good times we have had and now look how we after [sic] suffer for it. Do you remember how you loved to chase me around" (Lewis and Ardizzone, 98). In another letter to Leonard dated February 9, 1921, Alice writes,

> Just think of me, this evening being hear alone, mother and father and sister . . . as gone to the Westchester. . . . And I am hear alone, thinking of you, dear heart. I said to myself when they were going out, of the front door. I only wished Lenard was coming down this evening. How I could caress, you dear. . . . I went to bed, and stayed in my room, until five minutes to twelve, and got in bed, at twenty-five after I hopped in bed, and laid there, thinking of you, dear heart [sic]. (Lewis and Ardizzone 90)

Although both would be considered tame by modern standards, each of the excerpts above alludes to a shared sex life between Alice and Leonard. She feels comfortable referring to sex they had in the Marie Antoinette Hotel. Alice writes Leonard that she thinks of him when she is in bed and wishes to be alone with him in her home—the implication being for sexual reasons. In a third letter, Alice writes,

"But would it be awful if you had me my self alone. What you would not do to me. I can imagine..." (Lewis and Ardizzone 89). This letter further demonstrates that Alice receives pleasure from fantasizing about sexual contact with Leonard.

Clearly, Alice was open about her sexuality. Upon hearing the letters written between the two, the spectators of the trial could not pretend that female sexuality did not exist. Alice broke social guidelines by openly addressing her sexual desires and needs; even worse, those private desires became public for all the world to see, whether she wanted that or not. Sexually, Alice was an equal to her husband, rather than a subordinate, as was socially expected of her. In the 1920s, "[c]ommentators and social analysts still held that only unrespectable girls expressed themselves sexually outside the bounds of marriage. Love led to marriage, which provided the reason for sex. Women who had sex outside of marriage were perceived as somehow delinquent and the victims of their own desires" (Lewis and Ardizzone 147–8). In a sense, Alice had too much power. She was too much an equal participant in her sexual relationship with Leonard and was too comfortable with her own sexuality—and independent female sexuality was a frightening concept for many onlookers of the Rhinelander trial. Consciously or unconsciously, the balance needed to be restored to reassure onlookers that the social order was being maintained. By watching Alice undress, they stripped her of the power that she had in her relationship with Leonard, making her once again the acted upon, rather than the actor in her sexual life. Further, the trial reinforced the unfortunate stereotype of the degeneracy of the black woman.

Ultimately, *Rhinelander v. Rhinelander* had a lot to say about the proper roles of women, and specifically working-class black women. These three categories are intricately intertwined, and they are nearly impossible to separate. What is means to be a black woman is distinct from what it means to be simply be black, or to be a woman. Black women occupy a unique social position in which their race informs what society believes to be true about their womanhood and sexuality, and in which their sexuality affects their socially perceived level of "blackness." This case has as much to do with the proper sexual and romantic roles of men and women as it does with the roles of whites and blacks. Ultimately, the case exemplifies prevailing—and not completely resolved—stereotypes and attitudes about privilege, the underclass, race, and gender.

Bibliography

Lewis, Earl, and Heidi Ardizzone. *Love on Trial: An American Scandal in Black and White.* New York: W.W. Norton, 2001.

Marks, Michael J., and R. Chris Fraley. "Confirmation Bias and the Sexual Double Standard." *Sex Roles* 54.1-2 (2006): 19–26.

Onwuachi-Willig, Angela. "A Beautiful Lie: Exploring Rhinelander v. Rhinelander as a Formative Lesson on Race, Identity, Marriage, and Family." *California Law Review* 95.6 (Dec., 2007): 2393–458.

Papadaki, Evangelia. "Feminist Perspectives on Objectification." *The Stanford Encyclopedia of Philosophy.* Fall 2011. Web. 22 Apr. 2012. <http://plato.stanford.edu/entries/feminism-objectification/>.

Pappas, Stephanie. "Male Victims of Sexual Abuse Face Unique Challenges." *LiveScience.com.* TechMediaNetwork.com, 17 Feb. 2011. Web. 01 May 2012. <http://www.livescience.com/12909-senator-scott-brown-male-sexual-abuse-stigma.html>.

Smith-Pryor, Elizabeth M. *Property Rites: The Rhinelander Trial, Passing, and the Protection of Whiteness.* University of North Carolina, 2009.

Sonnen, Gloria. "Master-Slave Relationships." *Bowdoin College.* 15 Nov. 1999. Web. 22 Apr. 2012. <http://www.bowdoin.edu/~prael/projects/gsonnen/page4.html>.

index

Index